MICROSOFT PUBLISHER

2022

A Detailed Guide on Microsoft Publisher With Virtual Illustrations | Learn the Tips, Tricks and Shortcuts and Become a Pro in Few Days.

BENEDICT BONNY

Dedication

This book is dedicated to God almighty for his grace upon my life. And also, to my dad, Boniface and my late Mum, Edith Boniface for their impact in my life.

Table of Contents

Acknowledgement

I would like to express my special thanks of gratitude to God Almighty who gave me the strength and wisdom to write this book.

My special thanks go to John who kept late nights to ensure that this book was a success.

Also, I would like to express my thanks to my siblings; Stella, Kingsley, Rita for their support and encouragement.
Would it be fair if I failed to recognize the impact other members of my family and friends also played in making this book a success? Definitely not. Every of there support is what motivated me and kept me going all through to finalize this project within the time frame. Any attempt at any level can't be satisfactorily completed without the support and guidance of you guys.
Then again, I am overwhelmed in all humbleness and gratefulness to acknowledge my depth to all those who have helped me to put these ideas well above the level of simplicity and into something concrete.

Introduction

Welcome to the fantastic Publisher 2021, where you may experience everything from basic to expert level. This book was specifically prepared for individuals who are fortunate enough to utilize Publisher 2021, the newest and finest version.

Do you frequently find yourself writing for a newsletter, editing a newspaper, or starting new publications? You need Publisher, I see. Or perhaps you installed Microsoft Office on your computer, but you are just familiar with using Microsoft Word and Excel and have no idea what Publisher is or the many uses it serves as a powerful tool. In that case, this Publisher book is for you!

No longer does it matter whatever category you fit into, whether it was specified or not; the fact that you lay your lovely hands on the page and are reading it with these marvelous eyes is all the support you need! These simple yet generous pages provide all the information you want about Publisher, from the very beginning to the most expert level.

This book covers Publisher at all levels, from beginner to expert. I don't want to flaunt my grammatical skills in this book, so readers of all educational levels should be able to comprehend and enjoy every page, regardless of their level of knowledge. I'd also like to let you know that this book was written with a dash of humor to make the journey enjoyable and stress-free. At some time, you could be involuntarily grinning; if so, don't worry; you can't help it.

About This Book

This book has 15 chapters, and each one in-depth examines a magnificent feature of Publisher. You may open to any chapter and read it.

Each chapter is divided into discrete units, each of which is a subset of and related to the chapter's overall topic.

The chapter on Creating a Publication, for instance, contains gems like these:

- master pages or layout backdrops;
- adding contents, body, footers, dates, slide numbers, and logos;
- building custom layouts in the slide master view;
- preserving master page layout.
- producing and editing publications, creating master pages and layouts (and why to preserve)

You don't need to memorize or cram anything because this book has been so simply written and organized. Yes, unlike with other novels, you won't need to strain your head to understand this one.

Unwind; you're going to like this. Not everything in this book needs to be understood at once. It is a book that you consult when you have questions or want to confirm how to create a certain item on Publisher. For instance, you have tried every technique and still need to erase an empty publication from your publisher. If you already know how to do something but it isn't functioning, pick up this book and look into the section on Publications.

How to Use This Book

This book acts as a manual, source of information, and tutorial on everything related to Publisher.

Don't act hastily! You might start by researching a subject on your computer. Don't rush through this great dinner; instead, savor every bite slowly but thoroughly. Look up, grasp, and put into practice the page of the topic you wish to study from the table of contents!

Once you've found the page for the subject you want to research, take your time reading it and making sure you understand it. If you have to read a section several times to fully comprehend it; that's okay. Go practice the concept after you have it under control!

This book will serve as a reliable compass to guide you safely on whatever voyage you choose. It is packed with examples of workable instructions for managing Publisher at the professional level. If you're interested in learning how to erase an empty slide from your Publisher, read the chapter that discusses slides. You'll find the steps there.

Images that show you what you will see on your computer and how to understand a particular issue by simply following the instructions on and below the image are another exciting element that makes this book ideal for your enjoyment and simple comprehension. You may easily comprehend the many components of a Publisher interface and how they each work thanks to the photos.

Simple Presumptions

I have three presumptions regarding you. They are as follows:

- You have a computer, either a laptop or a desktop.

- You use Windows as your operating system.

- Publisher 2021 is something you either use or plan to use.

Please excuse my suppositions. I'm sorry to break it to you, but this book is for using PUBLISHER on Windows, not Linux, Chromium OS, FreeBSD, or any other operating system. If you are reading this, have a laptop, use Windows on your computer, and want to jump into the Publisher pool, Oh! Give me a fantastic hug, please!

Chapter 1

Welcome to Publisher 2021

In This Chapter

- Unraveling Microsoft Publisher
- Igniting Publisher
- Functionality of Publisher
- Creating a new publication
- Customizing Publisher Template
- Publisher Formatting Options
- Things to take note of and things to avoid

What Microsoft Publisher Can Do

Publisher

App

By fusing eye-catching text with eye-catching images, Microsoft Publisher lets you create anything.

Start with straightforward items like printed labels and cards. Gradually go on to more ambitious tasks including writing books, brochures, posters, newsletters, lesson plans, and wedding invites.

You may start with nothing. However, it's far simpler to begin with a design from Microsoft's extensive collection of templates. In this lesson for beginners, we'll begin with a pre-built template and then teach you the essential components to personalize it.

Using a Template to Launch a Publisher Document

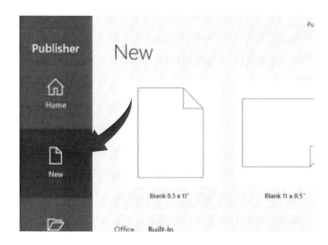

Creating a new publication from the templates available

Scroll down a bit and select Greeting Cards.

Go through the templates and select a Publisher template. In our example, we've picked a Birthday template.

Publisher Built-In Templates

The Microsoft Publisher has in it, amazing customized templates that can easily be used for publications of any kind. To use these amazing feature:

- Open the Publisher app

- Under the New Section, you then have the Built-In Templates as shown in the image below

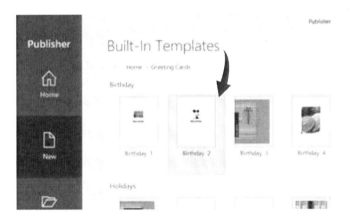

You can customize the template from the options on the right or do it later.

- Click on the Create button in the right pane.
- Once the template is open in Publisher, you can start formatting and editing it.

How To Customize a Publisher Template

The pages of any document display as thumbnails on the left side of Publisher. You can select any page and customize it.

In Publisher, everything is within boxes with borders. These are known as objects and they are like containers for every design element like text, lines, images, headers etc.

The boxes allow you to move those elements around the document to place them wherever you want.

You can change their characteristics easily, reorder them in a stack on top of each other, group them together, and even change their visibility.

For example, we shall modify the positions of the objects as shown in the image below:

- Once you click on the image or the text box, the image shows a rectangular box around it which you can use to either enlarge or decrease the size by expanding or compressing the nobs around the clicked image.

- You can also change the position of the option on the screen by clicking-down on it and moving it to the position of your choice and then removing your hand.

To understand it better, think about how you work with a simple Text Box in Microsoft Word. As this is a beginner's tutorial on Publisher, let's start by working with two of the most common elements in any design: Text and Pictures.

Add Text To Your Document

Templates have text boxes with dummy text. But you can always make your own.

To do this:

- Click **Home** on the **Ribbon** as shown below

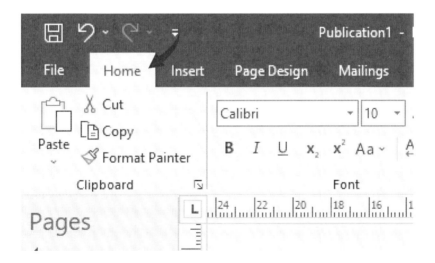

- **Click on the Draw Text Box** (In the Objects group) and drag the cross shaped cursor to draw a box where you want the text.

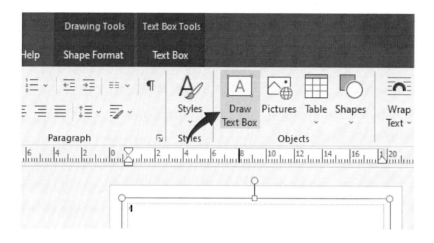

- **Type your text in the text box.** You can make the text box bigger by dragging the handles or link it to another text box. Publisher has a unique method of dealing with text that overflows.

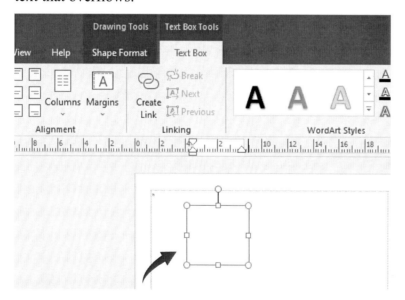

- A text box can also be edited. Texts already included in a text box can be edited as shown in the image below.

Text boxes can run out of space when they have too much text. A new text box can handle any text that overflows from the first. Text boxes can be connected. You can create new text boxes and make your content span more than one page or create columns of different widths. A little box with ellipses appears in the lower right of a text box when text overflows.

Add a fresh text box

When you click the ellipses in the first text field, a pitcher symbol appears. Click the new text box after moving there. The extra text will be shifted to the fresh text box.

The Windows typefaces that are used in Microsoft Word are also used in Publisher. Therefore, you must download and install fonts if you wish to utilize a unique typeface.

Include images in your document

To insert Images in your document:

- Click on the **Insert tab** as shown in the image below

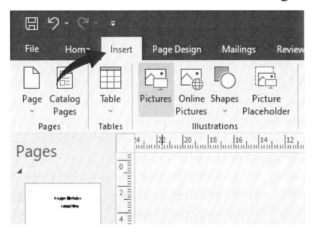

- In the **Illustrations group,** Click on **Pictures** to insert images from your PC

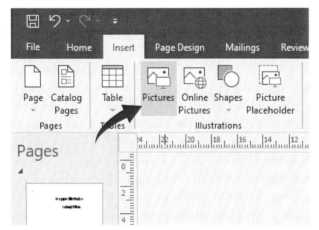

- To Insert images from the Online Source, click on the **Online Pictures** as shown below

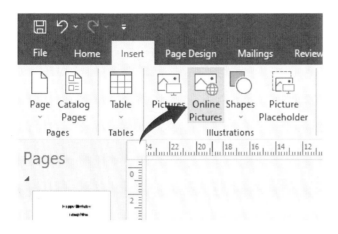

- You may create intriguing logos by combining straightforward forms from the **Shapes collection**.

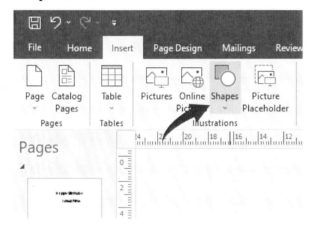

Utilizing Building Blocks, Add Elements

Building blocks are pieces that are already prepared and ready to "fit" into your design. These blocks may be modified and reused to fit your overall design. Headings, quotation forms, bars, borders, frames, calendars, and promotional material like coupons are a few examples of building blocks.

Building blocks make it easier for you to develop Publisher documents quickly. Any design component that you want to use again may be saved and used as a building block.

To Use this feature:

- Click on the **Insert tab** on the **Ribbon**

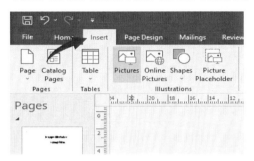

- Locate the **Building Blocks gallery** as shown in the image below

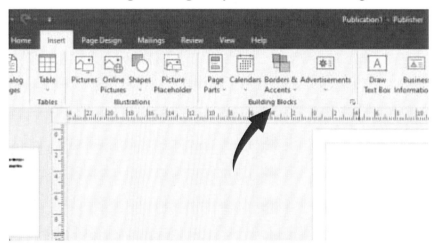

- **Click** on any **building block gallery** from the **four options** shown in the image below

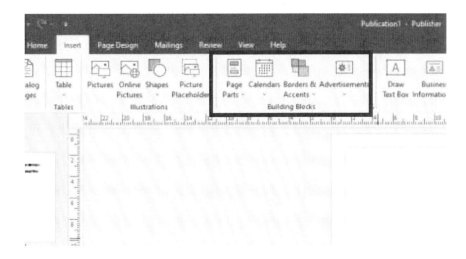

- **Choose** from the **options in the drop-down gallery** or select More [Building Block type] to discover whether the gallery contains any further options.

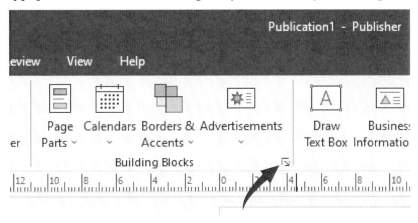

- To add any more building block to the document, click on it.

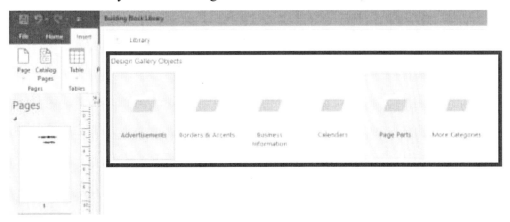

Remember, like any other element, you can drag the building block around on the page and manipulate it to fit your design. Building blocks are a combination of text, AutoShapes, and objects.

To quickly access their formatting options, right-click on the building block and choose Format from the menu.

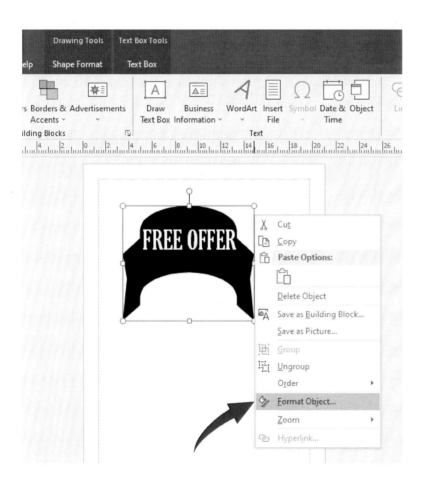

Check Your Document with the Design Checker

Microsoft Publisher is a desktop publishing program. So, in most cases, your final goal will be to print the document. Before you hit print, check the consistency of your layout with another Publisher feature called Design Checker.

To do this, follow the below procedures:

- Go to **File in the upper left corner** on your screen

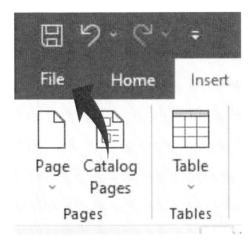

- Now, click on **Info**

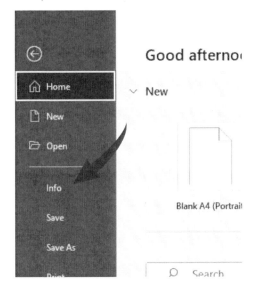

- Then, you will see, to your right hand side section, Click the clickable portion that says **Run design Checker.** On the same screen dsiplay, you have **Edit Business Information** section and the section to **Manage the Embedded Fonts**

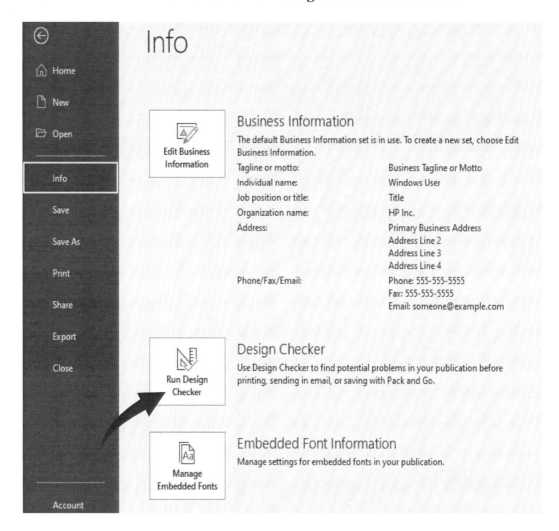

It's a troubleshooting step and saves you from printing mishaps. Click on Design Checker Options, and then select the Checks tab to see the many errors it tries to prevent as shown in the arrowed below.

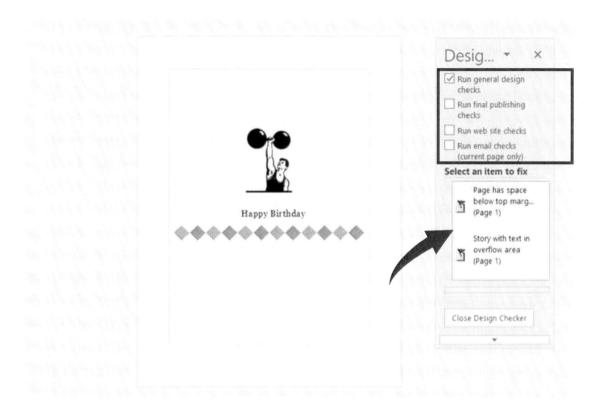

You can use this dialog to enable or disable the checks as boxed above.

Print Your Document

This is your final goal. But do note that you still have to print your content correctly on the type of paper you need for your project.

- Click **File**

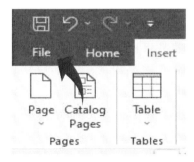

- Click on **Print**

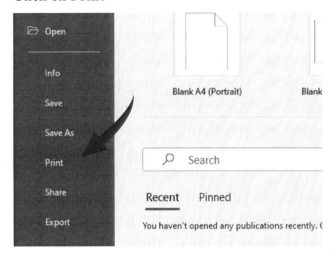

- On the Print screen, and enter a **number in the Copies** of print job box.

- **Choose the right printer**.

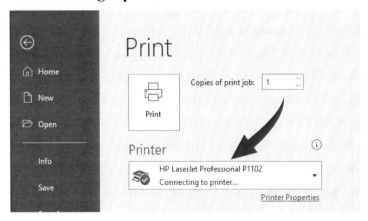

- Use the **Settings** according to the print job. It will differ with the type of document.

Export Feature in Microsoft Publisher

Microsoft Publisher also gives you a few Export options. To use this:

- Go to **File**

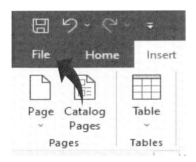

- Select **Export**.

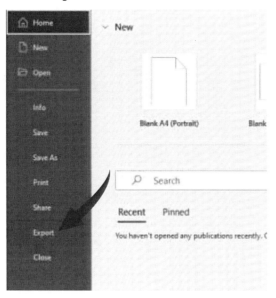

- There are three choices for you such as **Create PDF/XPS Document, Publish HTML and Change File Type** as shown in the image below

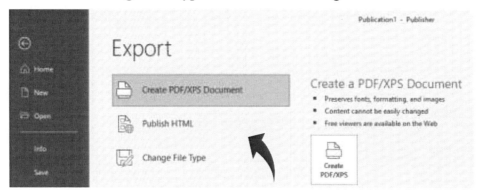

- There are three choices under **Pack and Go** if you want to save your document and export it for a printing run at a commercial press later. The Pack and Go Wizard packages your files and their assets like images, fonts, and colors into one file for commercial printing jobs

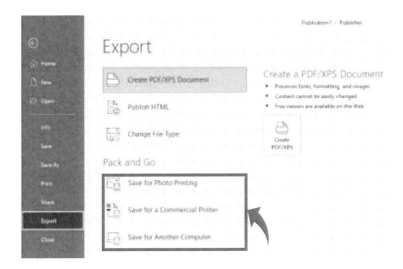

Workspace, Start Page and a Document Workspace Site (Cloud)

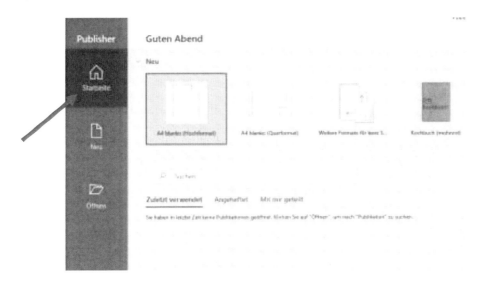

Go to the Start menu and select Microsoft Office- Microsoft Publisher from the application list to launch Microsoft Publisher. The main toolbar (known as a Ribbon) is located above the workspace screen, similar to other MS Office products. These two tabs, when clicked, open new Ribbons that undoubtedly deal with text and art/graphics, respectively.

Microsoft Publisher is a desktop publishing program that differs from Microsoft Word in that it focuses more on page design and layout than on text creation and editing.
Similar to Microsoft Word in that it focuses more on page layout and design and less on word composition and formatting, Microsoft Publisher is a graphic design program. In situations when employing other high end tools may not be practical, it offers small enterprises simple, affordable publishing choices for designing and creating logos.

One of the basic graphic design tools in Microsoft Office is called Microsoft Publisher. Because it is simple to use and doesn't require any prior understanding of the application or graphic design in general, it is said to be the best option for small businesses. Business cards, brochures, address labels, and calendars are just a few of the many basic business needs that Publisher supplies templates for Microsoft gives users the choice of sending a file directly via mail, exporting it as a different file format, or uploading it to the cloud and publishing it online.

A Document Workspace site is a SharePoint site that enables you to collaborate with other people on the creation of one or more related documents. The website offers facilities to share and update files as well as inform users of their status.

One can work directly in the file on the Document Workspace site or work on your own copy when you build a site that is based on files from any of the 2007 Microsoft Office system products, Publisher, Word, Excel, PowerPoint, or Visio. You can either update the server with changes from your copy or regularly update your own copy with changes from the server.

Your document is saved in the site's document library when you build a Document Workspace site, where users can access it using a web browser or edit with it using a Microsoft Office program.

Additionally, members can contribute relevant files to the library. On a SharePoint site, a library is a place where team members may create, gather, update, and manage files. File versions can be tracked by libraries so that users can view a history of changes and roll back to a previous version if necessary.

To stop users from making incompatible modifications at the same time, libraries can also require approval of files and the checking out of documents.

A Document Workspace site also offers lists, such as announcements and links, that aid in team communication and work tracking. For instance, you could want to offer a link to a relevant Web page or introduce a new team member who is working on the project. In order to receive an email whenever a document is changed or new information is added, you can sign up to receive notifications for the document or workspace.

Understanding Publisher 2021

Attractive, well laid out, and professionally prepared documents improve communication through the printed word. The work of generating newsletters, making brochures, developing advertisements, and other similar tasks used to be assigned to trained craftsmen. Today, a lot of this job is completed with the aid of computers and different software programs.

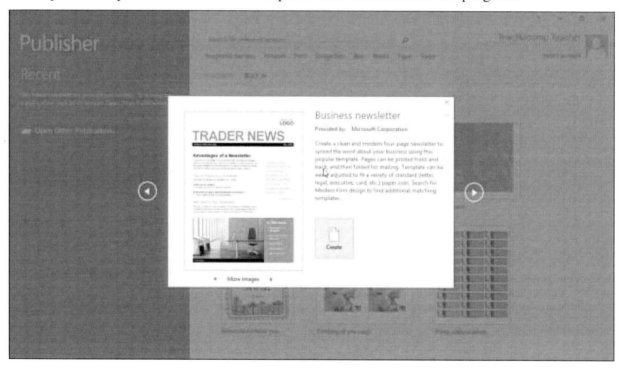

Publisher 2021 Overview

Expensive desktop publishing programs like PageMaker, Ventura, Quark Xpress, and InDesign are used to create complex documents quickly and efficiently. Previously, similar pages had to be manually created.

However, in order for these products to function properly, a high level of knowledge and competence is needed. Using them for the fast product advertisement, the social club flyer, or the company price list may be challenging and ineffective, but more significantly, it will waste time and money.

The easiest way to characterize Publisher is as a more capable desktop publishing software package's middle child. Even though it lacks some of the other packages' sophistication, it still includes the most of the functions. The main benefit is that it is simpler to utilize when making straightforward publications.

Uses Of Publisher

For usage at home, in small businesses, or even in corporations, Publisher is suitable. Here are a few examples of Publisher's potential applications:

- Product flyers
- Travel itineraries
- Price lists
- Product specials
- Notices

- Newsletters
- Bulletins
- Press releases
- Covers for manuals
- Letterheads
- Invitations
- Personalized greeting cards
- Posters
- Emails
- Company forms (e.g. invoices, stationery, order forms etc.)
- Photo albums

Starting Publisher In Windows 10

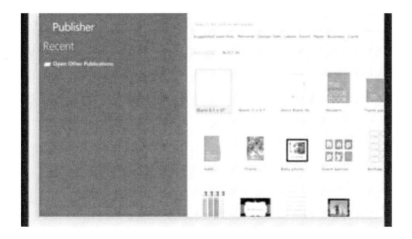

click this icon on the start screen on a windows system.

Start Publisher first before you may create or update a publication. The taskbar Search the web and Windows bar or the All apps list in the Start menu must be used to access Publisher for the first time.

The next time you use it, you may opt to pin it to the Start menu or the taskbar so that you can get to it more quickly and conveniently.

Try This Yourself:

Make sure your computer is turned on and the desktop is visible before you start.

- If the taskbar at the bottom of the desktop doesn't include a Publisher icon, click on the Windows icon there instead to bring up the Start menu.

- To get a list of every app on your computer, click on All apps. Navigate to the P section, where 2021's publishers are listed.

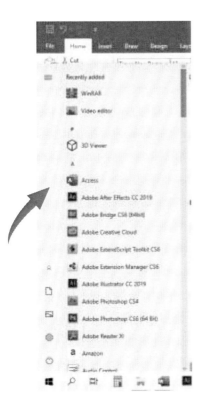

- To launch Publisher 2019, click on Publisher 2019. Select Pin this program to taskbar from the menu that appears when you right-click on the Publisher icon in the taskbar.

Now that you have clicked on this icon, Publisher will launch on your desktop. If you don't remove this icon from the taskbar, it will be there.

- To shut down Publisher, choose Close window. To reopen Project, click the Publisher icon in the taskbar.

To include a Publisher icon on the taskbar on your desktop:

1.   Open the Start menu and **select All Apps.**

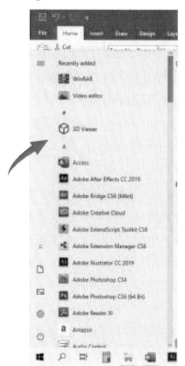

2.   Right-click Publisher 2021

3.   Choose "Pin to taskbar"

- To launch Publisher, click the Search... button in the taskbar, type publisher, and then select Publisher from the list of search results.

- To add Publisher 2019 to the Start menu, open the All Apps list, right-click on it, and **choose Pin to Start**

Understanding The Start Screen

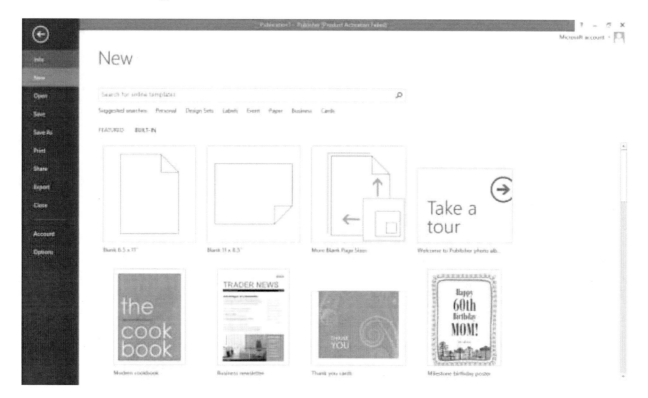

Usually, when you launch Publisher, a start screen appears. You can select the type of publication you want to work with from this opening screen. You have the option of working with one of your most recently viewed files, opening a previously made and saved publication, finding online templates, or producing a new publication using the provided templates.

Publisher 2021 Start Screen

you want to rapidly retrieve files you've recently worked on or start a new publication based on one of If the available templates, including the default Blank A4 (Portrait) publication template, the Publisher 2021 start screen is quite useful.

In the green pane to the left of the screen, under Recent, a list of recent files will appear if you have previously worked on a publication or several publications in Publisher. If you haven't yet worked on any publications, you can still open ones that are already open by selecting the link labeled "Open Other Publications," which is positioned beneath Recent. By doing this, you can access a previously saved file that was stored on your PC or OneDrive. The various templates for you to utilize when creating a new publication are shown as thumbnail previews in the primary pane of the Publisher start screen. The option for searching online templates is also included.

Templates are pre-designed templates that you can modify to meet your needs before adding pertinent content. Although you can start from scratch by selecting one of the Blank publishing templates, you'll usually find that working with templates that already have layouts in place is more convenient and saves time.

Publications are files produced by Publisher. Every publication made in Publisher is built using a template. A template outlines a publication's fundamental structure. Select a blank template to begin a straightforward publishing from scratch. Since blank templates are available in a variety of sizes, you can pick one that best meets your needs right away.

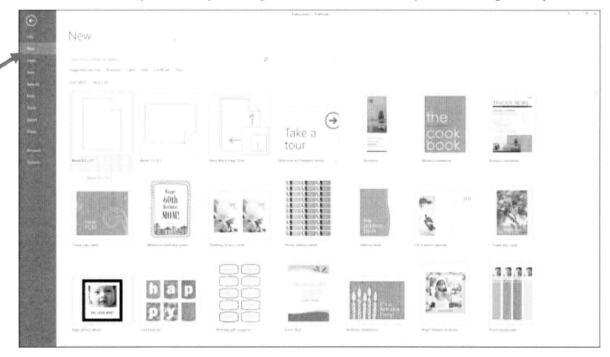

Make sure Publisher has launched and the Publisher start screen is visible before beginning this activity.

Check out the assortment of templates on the Publisher launch screen. Make sure FEATURED is chosen in the main window, as demonstrated. Toggle to Blank A4 (Portrait). The new publication will start out empty. The publication is given a temporary name by default, which is visible in the title bar.

A blank publication to be created:

1.   Launch Publisher to see the Publisher start screen

2.   Verify that FEATURED is chosen in the main pane.

3.   Select a Blank template from the list of templates by clicking on it.

To create a new publication while an existing one is open, click the File tab to get the backstage view, click on New, and then choose a Blank template. To show the Publisher start screen, press the + key on your keyboard.

The section where you create and edit your publications is called the Publisher screen. You will edit your publication using this screen, whether you start with a template or a blank one. Several important parts that make up the screen are discussed in detail on this page. The ribbon is one of these elements that appears in all Office programs.

The Backstage view, which provides file management features including saving, opening, shutting, printing, sharing, and more, is accessed through the File tab. Additionally, information like your document's properties is included here. You can also choose options to customize Publisher's working settings.

How Publisher Works

Three main sections make up the Publisher screen. Your input is shown on a page. Commands on the ribbon can be used to manipulate the data. The page is a component of a publication or file, an modifications to the publication or file are managed in backstage view. These essential elements are explained on this page.

The Page; The Pages navigation pane will appear on the left side of the screen when you create a new blank publication, and it will seem like a blank page in the publication window.

A template can also be used to produce a new publication; an example of one is the business newsletter on the right. The page with the template on it will show up in the publication window with the Pages navigation pane on the left, just like with a blank publication. You can update or add your own data to the specific information that will be displayed on the page by default.

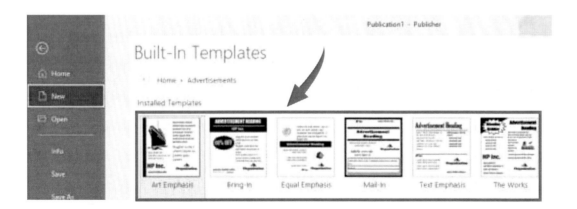

A ribbon; You can find all the necessary commands on the ribbon if you need to format, color, move, copy, or do anything else with the data on a page. The commands on the ribbon are arranged in a top row of tabs according to themes.

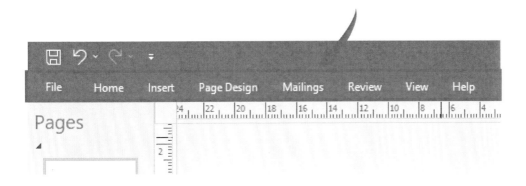

Backstage View

You must go to Publisher's Backstage view in order to perform actions on your publication, such as save it for later access, print it, share it with a colleague, or email it to your employer. The File tab on the ribbon can be used to access the Backstage view. Backstage takes up the entire screen and offers a series of options down the left side that let you carry out a number of tasks, as opposed to showing commands on a ribbon. The Print option is selected in our sample to the right, which is why you can see a preview of the publication and several print-related options on the screen.

The Ribbon

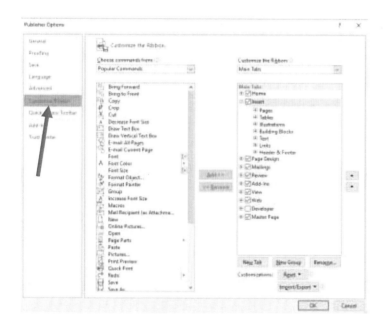

The primary tool you employ in Publisher is the Ribbon. It enables you to use every command offered by the program. There are tabs on the Publisher Ribbon. Different button sets of commands are contained in these tabs. Using the buttons, boxes, or menus present in each button group, you can access the commands contained within that group.

You can click the Dialog Box launcher button that displays in the lower-right corner of select button groups on the presently shown, or "active," tab within the Ribbon in Publisher to access advanced settings or for users accustomed to the traditional "dialog box" feature of Publisher. After doing so, a dialog box with choices for that button group appears.

Using The Ribbon

For Publisher, the command center is the ribbon. It offers a number of commands grouped into groups and displayed on pertinent tabs. To view the command groups, click on a tab's name to activate it. By clicking on a button, tool, or gallery option, commands are activated. This ribbon has a place for anything you might possibly want to accomplish in Publisher.

Put this to the Test: Make sure Publisher is running and you have a blank publication open before beginning this activity. Then;

- Examine the command groups listed on the **Home tab.** The majority of people utilize these commands.

- To add items like applications and media to your publication, select **the Insert tab** and use the commands there to construct pages, tables, drawings, building blocks, headers, and footers.

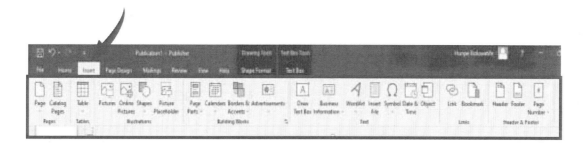

- To view the Shapes gallery, select **Shapes** from the **Illustrations group**. A wide variety of shapes are featured in this collection.

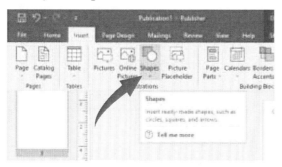

- Check out the commands by clicking on each tab. Several of these visible "dialog boxes". To open the Change Template dialog box, click the **Page Design tab**, then click **Change Template in the Template group.**

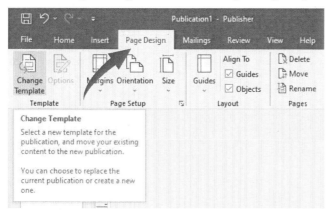

- Click on [Cancel], then click on the [Home tab]

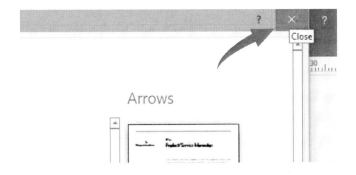

To use the ribbon:

1. Click on a tab to display the commands

2. Click on a button to activate a command, display a gallery or display a dialog box

Contextual tabs are additional tabs that show up on the ribbon in particular situations. For instance, the Picture Tools: Format tab will show up if you insert a picture. All the tools you could need to edit and work with an image are now easily accessible.

Collapsing the ribbon;

*   In the ribbon's bottom right corner, click Collapse the Ribbon.

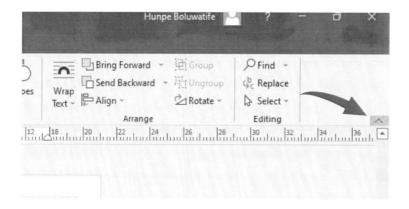

- In the ribbon's bottom right corner, click Pin the Ribbon to make it visible.

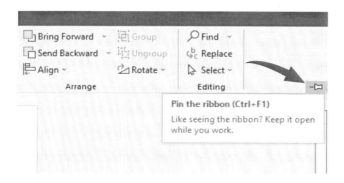

- Press + or double-click on any tab (except from the File tab) to swiftly collapse the ribbon so that it only shows the tab names. The ribbon can be expanded once more by using these features.

With the ribbon, you may edit a publication's content in a variety of ways, including by adding new text, formatting it, including images, copying it, and more. You can interact with the file you generate by going to the Backstage view, which is accessible from the File tab. You can email it, print it off, and save it for later use, among other options.

The File tab on the ribbon is different from other tabs since it is colored, as can be seen from the backstage view. When you select the File tab, Microsoft Publisher's Backstage view mini-program starts up. The entire screen is taken up by Backstage, as it is commonly referred to.

A navigation pane with tabs is located to the left of Backstage. You have access to a number of functions through these tabs, including printing, saving, and sharing. Additionally, they can give you details about your publishing, such the file size.

When one of these tabs is clicked, a number of options related to the selected operation are displayed. Back stage's main objective is to protect your data, enable you share it with others, and give you useful data about your publication. The Info tab may display various information depending on the publication's type and any modifications made to it.

Summary of using The Ribbon

At the top of the Publisher window is the Ribbon, which is separated into tabs.

- The selected, or "active," tab in Publisher's Ribbon contains the program's commands.

- Click one of the Ribbon tabs to change the button groups that are visible in Publisher.

- Click the corresponding buttons, boxes, or menus in the button group to utilize the commands on the active tab.

- Click the "Dialog Box" launcher button in the lower-right corner of a button group to open a dialog box for the button groups that have that option.

- Double-click the currently active tab on the Ribbon in Publisher to reveal or hide its contents.

- When you choose a specific type of publication object from the Ribbon, additional "contextual" tabs will show up in addition to the main tabs that are already available to you. When you choose a picture, table, text box, or piece of WordArt on a publication page, contextual tabs emerge. The button groups that afterwards show up on the contextual tabs are closely related to the kind of object that was chosen.

- Click away from the chosen object in the publication window to remove contextual tabs from Publisher's Ribbon.

Backstage Tabs

More possibilities for interacting with a publication can be found in the Backstage tabs:

- **Information;** Allows you to control versions and permissions and provides status information about the current publishing.

- **New;** enables you to build a new magazine and offers fast access to a variety of online templates in addition to a gallery of built-in templates.

- **Open;** Gives you the choice to search your computer, OneDrive, or another location to find what you're searching for, as well as a list of recent publications.

- **Save;** asks you to save to a location or saves your current publication (if it hasn't previously been saved to one).

- You may give your publication a name and a location by using the **Save As** function.

- **Print;** enables you to print and see the most recent publication. Allows you to send your publication to others as a PDF or XPS file via email.

- **Export;** Provides options for saving and printing, as well as the ability to publish as a PDF, XPS, or online publication.

- **Close;** ends the publication you're reading.

- **Account:** Contains user and product data. Offers you a variety of alternatives that will help with the production and editing of your publication.

You can work on your publications and access important details about the Publisher status from the Backstage view. It can be accessible by clicking on the File tab, which is located to the left of the ribbon, but it can also be accessed by using keyboard shortcuts for particular operations.

Make sure Publisher is running and that you have a blank publication open before beginning this activity.

- To view the Backstage, select the **File tab**. To access details about your publication, such as the Properties, make sure Info is selected in the left green window.

- To view your printing options, **click Print**. An illustration showing how the article will look when printed.

- To view the account choices and product license details, click on **Account**. To close Backstage and return to the publication, click on the Back arrow at the top of the green pane.

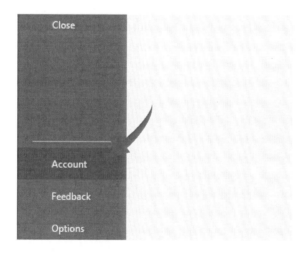

Getting to the Backstage:

1.   Select the **"File" tab.**

2.   In the green panel on the left side of the screen, click the desired tab. Backstage can be closed by pressing.

The bar that runs the length of the Publisher window's bottom is the status bar. It is a helpful tool that shows data like the current page number and specifics about a chosen object.

You can **zoom in and out** of the page as well. There are tools to adjust the publication view in the status bar. The information displayed in the status bar can be changed through customization.

Page Number: The page number identifies which page is currently being shown and how many pages are in the book. The Pages navigation window can be opened and closed by clicking on the page number.

Object Position: The Object Position shows the coordinates for the presently selected object's current location. When you click on the Object Position, the Measure dialog box will popup, allowing you to change the selected object's measurements. The Object Position will show the mouse pointer's current location coordinates if no object is currently selected.

Object Size: This option shows the size of the object that is currently selected. The Measure... dialog box will popup when you click on Object Size, just like with Object Position.

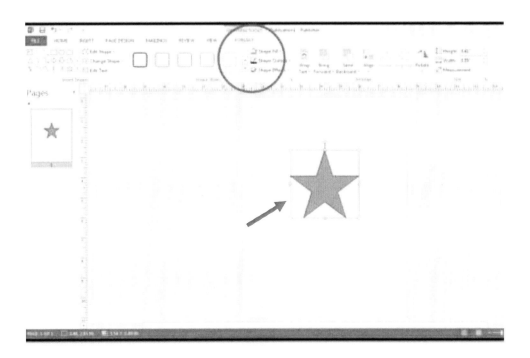

Layout Tools: These tools let you alter how the publication appears to you. The publication can be seen as either a Single Page or a Two-Page Spread. Zoom Slider: The zoom slider shows the current zoom level, with the center mark denoting 100%. To change the zoom percentage, either move the marker to the left or right or click on a specific spot on the slider. Additionally, you can zoom in or out by clicking on the plus or minus sign at either end of the slider.

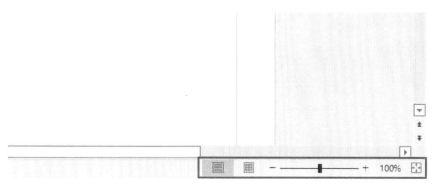

Zoom Level: The percentage of current zoom is shown by this button. The Zoom dialog box will open when you click the button, allowing you to choose a specific zoom level.

Show Entire Page; The zoom is adjusted such that the complete current page is seen in the window when you click Show Whole Page. The status bar's contents can change drastically. If the one on your screen differs somewhat from the sample above, don't be frightened.

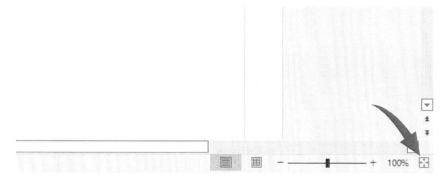

You may modify your status bar by right-clicking the status bar itself and choosing the additional tools you want to add from the shortcut menu.

To avoid losing your work and maybe harming your computer, you must exit Publisher carefully after you have done working on a publication. Publisher includes a unique exit command that you should utilize, much like other Windows-based programs. If you haven't previously, you will typically be prompted to save your work.

Make sure Publisher is running and that you have a blank publication open before beginning this activity.

- **Name in the box;** Your name will be at the top left corner of a text box that spans the entire page. Your publication has changed as a result of doing this, therefore if you try to depart, you will be given the option to save. In Publisher's upper right corner, select Close. If you want to keep your data, you will now be prompted to save your publication. You will receive a message that resembles the one displayed. We won't bother saving this publication because we have no need to maintain it.

- **Press [Don't Save]** to leave Publisher 1 now. In the Publisher window's upper right corner, select Close. If you want to save your modifications, click [Save], then provide the name and location of the publication. If not, click [Don't Save].

- You can terminate Publisher by keybinding.

Function Of Microsoft Publisher

Microsoft Publisher UI

You have access to a variety of tools in the publisher drawing toolbar to create a limitless number of images. In Publisher, you can enter text directly on the text frame or with different text that is exactly as it is in any formatting, and then send it or export it to a word processor because it has the format painter feature that is not available in any other DTP package. You can even prepare an arrow that is also available in PageMaker. All of the fonts associated to the windows are automatically available in this.

TMS Publisher is used seldom today, although it was once widely used because it is a part of MS Office and does not need to be purchased separately. It is also simple to learn because the majority of its rules and procedures are the same as those of MS Office, most notably MS

Word. People who are proficient with MS Word and I can work on that can quickly learn MS Publisher from the beginning.

You need to have highly advanced knowledge of MS Publisher's benefits.

If working with MS-Office comes naturally to you, learning this will also be simple. This is also quite simple for someone who is brand new to learning.

The other DTP packages are available in addition to these well-known ones, and each has its own unique strengths and weaknesses. In this portion, we have focused on the Microsoft Publisher.

What Microsoft Publisher can do?

The features offered by Microsoft Publisher are as follows:

1. Effects for letters, shapes, and photos at a high technical level.

2. The option to use backdrop images of high quality.

3. Tools for mail merging.

4. Tools for personalization.

5. Photo import and exchange through drag and drop.

Other functions include:

- For accurate measurements, use the detailed ruler and instructions.

- Shareable document capabilities.

- Microsoft Publisher's capabilities

- The publisher is a helpful piece of desktop publishing software.

- It lets you control elements like page size, text, pictures, and borders.

- One of Publisher's strengths is its capacity to combine text and images to create flyers, brochures,

- handouts, and newsletters that seem polished.

Chapter 2

Your First Publication!

In This Chapter

- Unraveling Microsoft Publication
- Understanding & Planning Publication
- Impact on Publication Design
- Accessing Publisher Template
- Inserting & Formatting Text
- Adding & Editing Business Information
- Previewing & Printing a Publication

Unraveling Microsoft Publication

The ability to create a new publication is pivotal to working successfully within Publisher. There are several basic skills you will need to master in order to achieve this. These include being able to type and edit text, work with objects, print, and the ability to save information for future use (not necessarily in that order). In this session you will:

1. Gain an understanding of how to plan a publication
2. Gain an understanding of publication types
3. Learn how to add and edit business information
4. Learn how to create a publication from a template
5. Gain an understanding of the save as place
6. Gain an understanding of the save as dialog box
7. Learn how to save a new publication
8. Learn how to insert text
9. Learn how to format text
10. Learn how to undo and redo actions in a publication

11.   Learn how to save an existing publication

12.   Learn how to view a preview of a publication

13.   Learn how to print a publication

14.   Learn how to close a publication safely.

While it may be tempting to start creating a publication without planning it first, thinking about what you want to create before you get started will save you time and energy later on. Without a clear idea of your intentions and requirements, you may find yourself making changes that you otherwise would not have had to make, and end up with an unsatisfactory publication.

Impact on Publication Design

Purpose

Identify what you are trying to achieve with this publication. Are you trying to provide information, persuade people to make a decision or choice, motivate or inspire individuals or teams, or set up a web page for reference purposes? The purpose of your publication will determine its framework.

Theme

Once you decide on the purpose of your publication, it is important to choose a design that complements and is appropriate for that purpose. For example, a template with bright colors and pictures might be great for communicating the new plans for a children's classroom or childcare center, but would be inappropriate for an accountant's annual report.

Audience

Consider who you are designing the publication for. Are they knowledgeable about the subject or complete novices? What is their age, background, location and position in the company? The design and language that you use must reflect on who you are trying to communicate with.

Key Ideas

Consider what the most important idea that you are trying to communicate is. What other ideas do you introduce that are also key to the success of the publication? These ideas must be the primary focus of your publication and presented in a way that demands the attention of the audience.

Action Required

Consider what action you want to take place as a result of your publication. Do you want people to support your proposal? Do you want feedback on the information you have provided? Maybe you need to include details that provide a plan of action or contact information.

Time Frame

The amount of time you have to complete the publication has a significant impact on how you can prepare it. Do you have time to be pedantic about the graphics or do you need something out in a hurry? Will you create your own design, or settle on a standard design and allow more time to prepare the content?

Stationery

Consider the type of stationery you are planning to use. Do you require special paper or pre-scored cards? Do you have them in stock? Do you have labels that you need to match the dimensions of?

Form of Publication

If you need matching sets of publications, think about what you need overall.

Are you looking to create a greeting card, flyer, tri-fold A4 page or letterhead with matching envelopes? If you can't find exactly what you have in mind in one template category, you may find that you can use a template for a different type of publication for your project. For example, a top fold card will create pages that are exactly one quarter of an A4 page. You could use these to create four identical images on one sheet of paper.

Publisher provides you with a large assortment of templates that you can use to create various types of publications. These templates can be accessed from the New place in the Backstage and have been organized into different sections in order to make them easier to navigate.

Accessing Publisher Templates

You can access Publisher templates by either displaying the Publisher start screen, or clicking on the

File tab, then clicking on New. Within the New place, templates have been organized into two sections – FEATURED and BUILT-IN. The FEATURED section is designed to provide you with easy access to templates that you use regularly. It contains an assortment of blank template options as well as commonly used templates, and any templates that you have used recently. The FEATURED section is a good starting place if you use the same template on a regular basis (for instance, if you publish a monthly newsletter), or if you need to create a publication of a high standard quickly and easily; however, your choices are limited by the range that is supplied, and you risk displaying a lack of personal creativity by following strongly defined styles. This section will not display if you are not connected to the internet.

The BUILT-IN section differs from the FEATURED section, as rather than displaying thumbnail previews of particular templates, it displays a list of categories of different types of publications.

These categories are listed alphabetically so that you can easily find the type of publication you are looking for. Clicking on a category will display thumbnail previews of templates based on the category they belong to. For example, clicking on the Award Certificate category will display an array of different award certificate templates with different layouts.

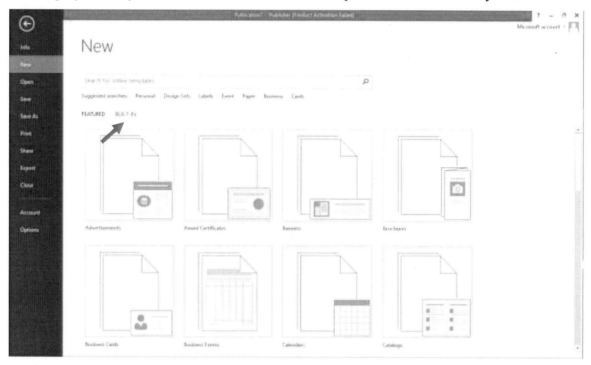

If you cannot find the appropriate template for your publication under either FEATURED or BUILT IN, you may wish to search for more online. You can use the Suggested searches options to find other Brochure, Label, Card, Certificate, and Flyer ideas, or you can use the Search for online templates box to search for something more specific.

BUILT-IN Categories

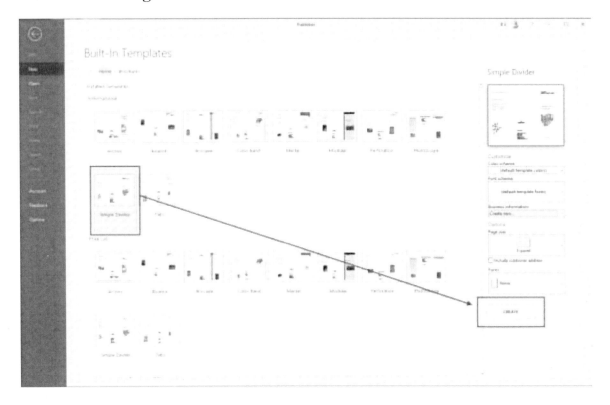

Figure: The BUILT-IN Categories

The BUILT-IN section contains an alphabetically ordered list of 26 different template categories, which are listed below. Some of these categories in turn contain a list of subcategories (for example, the Brochures category contains Informational, Price List, Event and Fundraiser subcategories), as well as standard blank templates and blank templates sorted by stationery provider (allowing you to ensure your publication exactly fits the stationery you will be printing it on). The templates stored in these subcategories can be edited and modified in a variety of ways.

- Advertisements
- Envelopes
- Newsletters
- Award Certificates

- Flyers
- Paper Folding Projects
- Banners
- Gift Certificates
- Postcards
- Brochures
- Greeting Cards
- Programs
- Business Cards
- Import Word Documents
- Quick Publications
- Business Forms
- Invitation Cards
- Resumes
- Calendars
- Labels
- Signs
- Catalogues
- Letterhead
- With Compliments Cards
- E-mail
- Menus

Whereas the other 25 types are known as Publications for Print, E-mail designs are typically for use in an online environment and are therefore structured somewhat differently.

Adding And Editing Business Information

Publisher can hold a record of your personal or business details – name, organization, address, phone, e-mail and the like. Once it is saved as a Business Information Set, you can then enter this information automatically into any publication you create. If you are signed in with your Microsoft Account, Publisher may automatically import information from there for your information set.

Before starting this exercise, ensure Publisher has started...

1. Create a blank publication, then click on the Insert tab

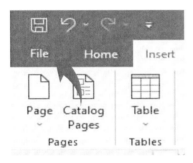

2. Click on Business Information in the Text group, then select Edit Business Information to display the Create New Business Information Set dialog box

If the Business Information dialog box is displayed instead, click on [New] to display the Create New Business Information Set dialog box

3. Select the text in Individual name, type Jim Wallis, then complete the dialog box as shown

4. Click on [Add Logo] to display the Insert Picture dialog box

5. Navigate to the course files folder, click on Alpheius Logo.jpg, then click on

6. Click on [Save] to display the Business Information dialog box

7. Click on [Close] to close the dialog box and return to the publication

For Your Reference

To create a business information set:

1.   Click on the Insert tab, then click on **Business Information** in the Text group

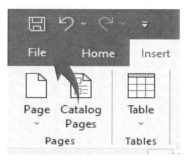

2.   Select Edit Business Information, then fill out the details as required

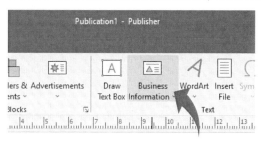

3.   Click on [Save], then click on [Update Publication] or [Close]

The Business Information dialog box enables you to create new profiles or edit current profiles.

Clicking on [Update Publication] will update the publication with the details from the currently selected business information set.

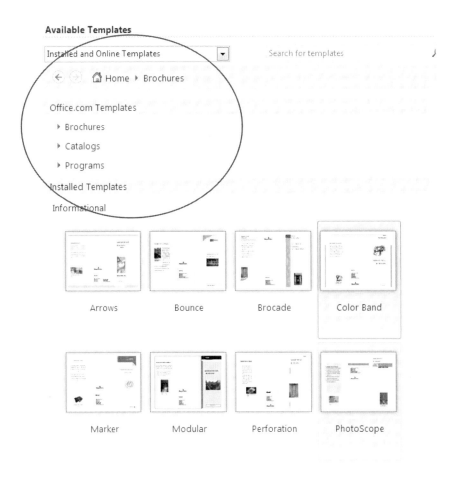

Creating A Publication From A Template

Figure: Creating a Publication from Installed and Online Templates

Publisher provides you with a range of different templates to make creating effective publications quick and simple. All you need to do is select the template that will best suit your needs. Once you have chosen a template, you can modify aspects of the publication such as the color scheme and the font scheme.

Continue using the previous file with this exercise, or open a new, blank publication.

1.   Click on the **File tab**, click on New, then click on **BUILT-IN** to view the categories of locally stored templates

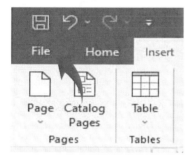

2.   **Click on [Brochures]** to display thumbnail previews of built-in brochure templates

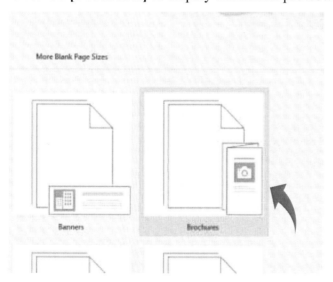

3.   Click on [Bars] under More Installed Templates to select this template

4.   In the right pane, click on the drop arrow for **Color scheme**

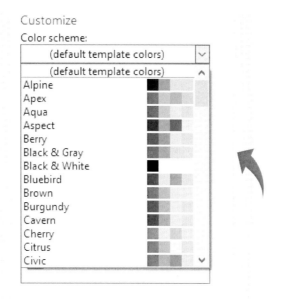

5.   Scroll down to and **click on [Moss] to apply** this color scheme

61

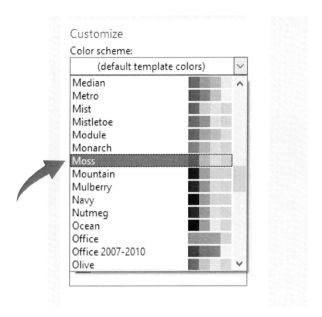

Notice that all of the thumbnails are updated to demonstrate the selected color scheme...

6.   Click on [CREATE] to create a new brochure based on the Bars template

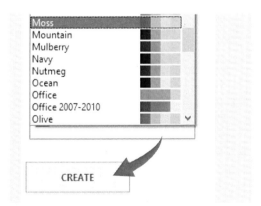

Notice that the [JW_Work] business information set is used by default

To create a publication:

1.   Click on the [File tab], then click on [New]

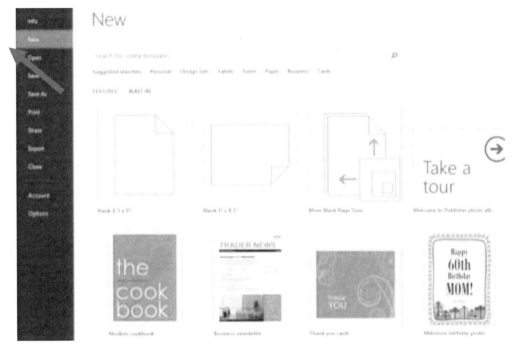

Figure: The FEATURED Templates when creating a new publication

2.   Select a **category**

Figure: Template Categories for creating a new publication

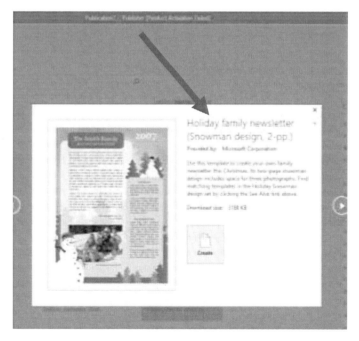

3.   Select a publication design, if available

4.   Adjust the other settings using the right pane, then click on [Create]

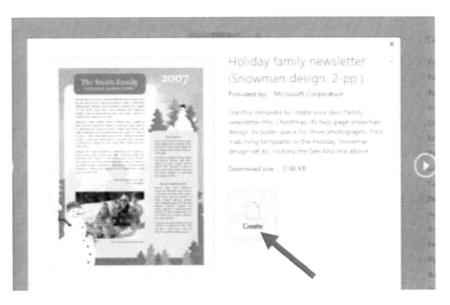

In addition to the templates that are built in to Publisher, you can download more templates for free from Office.com.

Pictorial Representations of the steps in creating a Publisher file from templates.

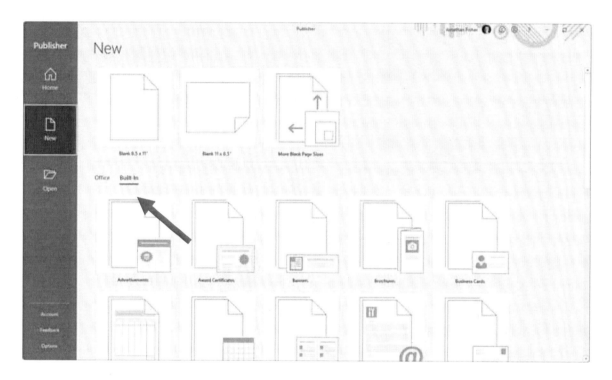

Step 1: Over the shown templates, select the **Built-In tab.**

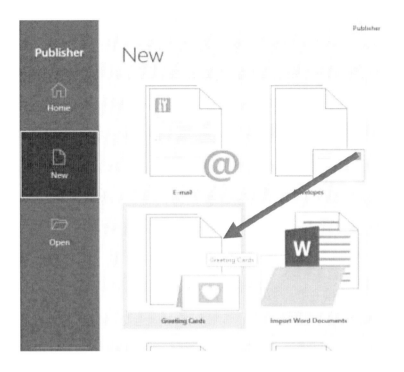

Step 2: Select **Greeting Cards** by a little bit scrolling down

Step 3: From the Birthday section up there, pick a template.

Step 4: Choose **Create** in the right pane.

The Save As Feature

The [Save As] place will display when you open the Backstage and click on Save As. It gives you easy access to locations (known as places in Office) where you can save your publications, such as the folders on your computer or OneDrive, and provides you with the option of adding other places to save your publications to, such as SharePoint.

The [Save As] place displays automatically when you choose to save a new publication for the first time by clicking on the File tab and clicking on Save. The Save As place will also display if you save an open, existing publication to a new storage location by clicking on the File tab and clicking on Save As. The Save As place lists storage places in the middle pane of the Backstage so they are easily accessible. By default, Microsoft lists OneDrive at the top of the list. When you click on either OneDrive or This PC, a list of recently accessed folders in that place will appear in the right pane, as well as the option to [Browse] the folders.

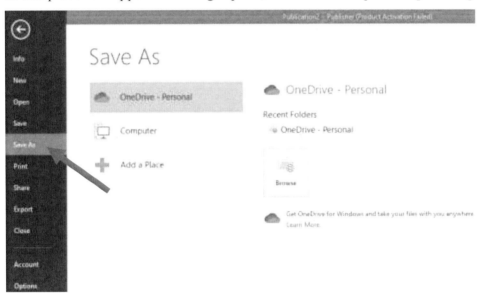

OneDrive

An Overview

Microsoft runs the file hosting service OneDrive (formerly SkyDrive). It was first introduced in August 2007 and allows registered users to synchronize and share their data. Microsoft Office's web based storage backend is likewise powered by OneDrive. OneDrive provides 5 GB of storage space without charge; further storage capacities of 100 GB, 1 TB, and 6 TB are also offered, either independently or as part of Office 365 subscriptions.

The OneDrive client software gives its device file syncing and cloud backup capabilities. For macOS, Android, iOS, Windows Phone, Xbox 360, Xbox One, and Xbox Series X and S, as well as Microsoft Windows, the software is included. Furthermore, Microsoft Office applications have a direct integration with OneDrive.

Function of OneDrive in Publisher

OneDrive, or OneDrive.com, is an online file storage system hosted by Microsoft. Currently, Microsoft provides you with 7GB of free cloud storage (or 20GB for Office 365 users) on OneDrive to store your files and photos, sync files across your computers or storage devices, share specific files with friends and colleagues, and edit and collaborate on Office files. You can access the latest version of your files from any device with an internet connection, including mobile devices. You can also create new files directly in OneDrive.

Before you can upload files to OneDrive, you will need to create a Microsoft account (which you will be prompted to do the first time you try to save a file to OneDrive). From then on you can go to OneDrive and sign in with your Microsoft account to access, view and share your online files.

Adding A Place

By default, the Save As place lists your OneDrive and This PC as places you can save your publications to. However, you also have the option of adding SharePoint to this list. Clicking on Add a Place beneath Save As will open a dialog box that will take you through the steps necessary for adding SharePoint. Once it is added, SharePoint will appear in your list of available places.

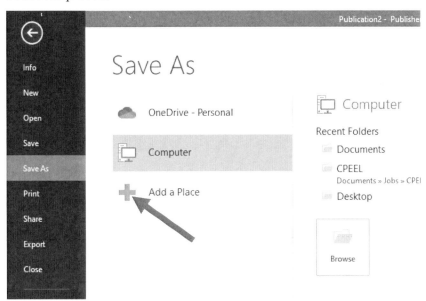

Current Folder

If you have been working with a publication that has already been saved to a folder, the Save As place will remember the location and display it under Current Folder at the top of the right pane so that you can easily access it.

Recent Folders

If you have been working with publications stored in various folders, these folders will be listed under Recent Folders in the right pane. You can save your publication to one of these folders by clicking on it under Recent Folders and the Save As dialog box will open with that folder already selected. By default, five folders will display under Recent Folders. However, you can change this by clicking on Options in the Backstage and clicking on Advanced. Under Display, set the number of recent folders you wish to display between 0 and 20.

List of available storage places

The Save As Dialog Box

Once you have created a publication, it is vital that you save it if you plan to keep it. By saving a publication, you move the information from temporary memory to a source of more permanent memory (such as the computer's hard drive). To save the publication you must access and use the Save As dialog box, as described below.

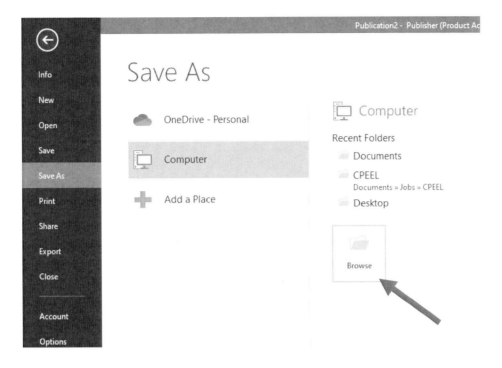

Finding a Folder

No matter where you want to save your publication, you will have to use the Save As dialog box. This dialog box allows you to choose a name for your publication and the location in which you wish to store it so that you can easily access the publication again. The Navigation pane, located on the left side of the dialog box, enables you to browse through the files and folders in your computer or OneDrive in order to choose an appropriate location in which to save your publication.

When you point to the Navigation pane, some folders will display a small, light grey, right-pointing arrow – this indicates the folder contains subfolders. When you click on this arrow, the folder will expand to display a hierarchy of subfolders. The arrow will then change to a small, dark grey, down pointing arrow.

Click on a drive or a folder in the Navigation pane to identify the folder in which you want to save the file. The current contents of the folder will display in the pane to the right of the dialog box.

You can also use the Address bar at the top of the dialog box to move up or down one or more levels in the folder structure if desired. To do this, simply click on the name of the folder you wish to open in the Address bar. For instance, in the example below clicking on Documents in the Address bar would take you back to the Documents folder.

Address bar Navigation pane

The contents of the folder you have selected in the Navigation pane will display here (the Publications folder in our case)

Saving A New Publication On Your Computer

Few things are more frustrating in the world of computers than doing an hour's work and then losing it all because the computer crashes. This is one reason why it is important to save your work regularly. Saving your work moves the information from the computer's short-term memory (known as RAM), to long-term memory such as the hard drive so you can access it again later.

Same File

Continue using the previous file with this exercise, or open the file Publication Tutorial File_1.pub.

- Click on the File tab, click on Save As, then ensure This PC is selected.
- Click on [Browse] to open the Save As dialog box
- Type Brochure in File name
- Click on Local Disk (C:) under This PC in the Navigation pane to display the folders on the C: drive. The list of folders will appear in the pane on the right…
- Double-click on Course Files for Microsoft Publisher 2019 in the right pane
- Click on [Save] to save the publication to the Course Files folder

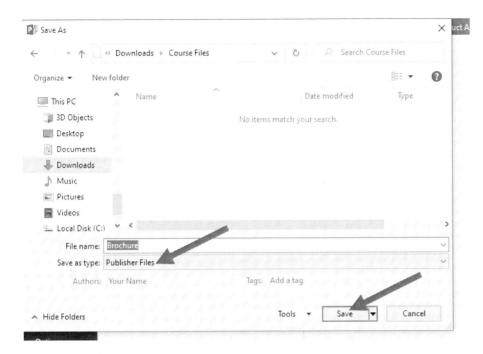

Notice the new name appears in the title bar at the top of the screen

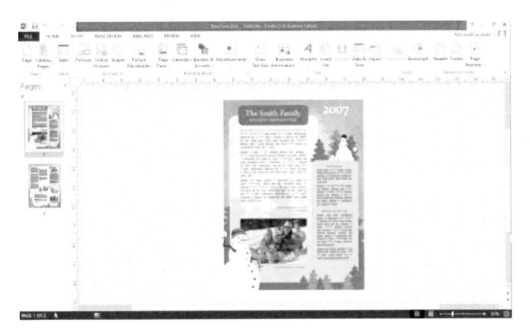

To save a publication:

1.   Click on the **File tab,** then navigate to the Save As dialog box

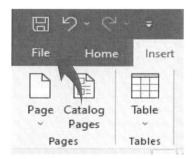

2.   Click **Save** and locate the desired **save** location

3.   Type a File name, then click on **[Save]**

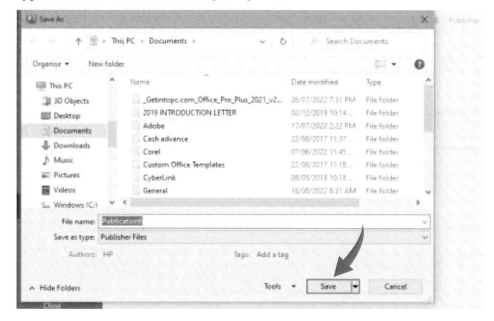

- You can press the keyboard shortcut + or click on Save in the Quick Access Toolbar to quickly save a publication.

Inserting Text

Most publications that you create will require you to enter text, whether it be a heading, an article or a price list. In Publisher, text must be entered into a text box. The vast majority of the templates provided by Publisher already have text boxes in them, allowing you to simply replace the default

placeholder text with your own information.

To insert text:

1. Click in the **text box** or the existing text that you want to replace

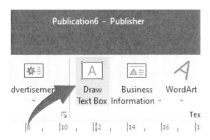

2. Type the desired text

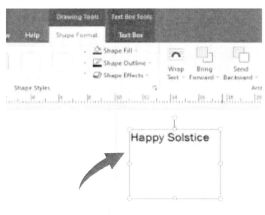

Options for modifying text boxes are available in the Format Text Box dialog box, which you can access by clicking on the dialog box launcher in the Text group on the Text Box Tools: Format tab.

Formatting Text

Creating Bulleted and Numbered Lists

You can make a variety of lists that are incredibly straightforward and simple to remember. Numbered lists have numbers, while bulleted lists contain bullet points. We'll discover how to produce both.

Select the text you want to use to construct a list from a text box if you want to add it to an existing body of text.

The text that we wish to convert into a list has been chosen in the example below.

After that, select the Home tab and then select the "Paragraph" group. According to your needs, choose the numbered list or the bulleted list button from the options shown below.

(You'll see that the first button is for a list with bullets, and the second is for a list with numbers.)

We went with bullets.

A bullet style can be selected from a dropdown menu.

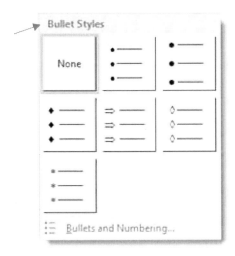

The bullets are added to your list.

If you're making a new list:

- Place the cursor where you wish to make the list in the publication.

- Select the numbered or bulleted list button.

- Start typing.

A numbered list like the one above is one.

Paragraph Alignment

You may align your text and paragraphs to the left, the right, the center, or the justify-option, as with many word processing systems. You can use one of these strategies to the whole publication or just a certain passage of text.

This is an example of text that is aligned to the left.

                                This is text that is aligned to the right.

                   This text is centered.

The content that follows, which is taken from this session of the book, is justified so that it is placed within the left and right margins, with extra space if required between the characters. It provides the magazine a polished appearance.

The following text, selected from this lesson, is justified so that it is aligned between the left and right margins, adding space between letters if necessary. It gives the document a clean look.

The Home tab's Paragraph group contains the buttons or instructions for text alignment, as seen in the illustration below.

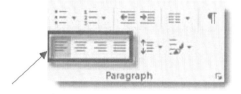

Left Align, Center Align, Right Align, and Justify are the options from left to right.

Simply choose a formatting strategy, as we discussed in the last part, and click the corresponding button to employ them.

Setting Line Spacing

Line spacing refers to the amount of white space that appears between each line of text in a paragraph. Each line has a gap added by the publisher.

Navigate to the Paragraph group under the Home tab to adjust line spacing. Click the button.

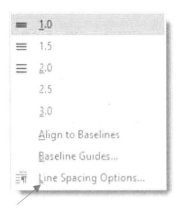

Values for line spacing will then appear. Double space is denoted by 2.0. A single space is represented by 1.0. Click Line Spacing Options if you don't see the desired spacing.

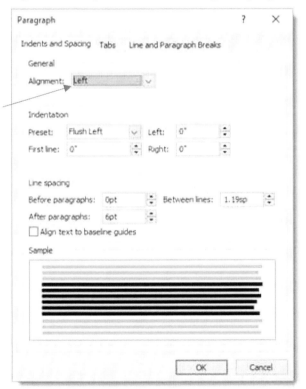

Go to the Line Spacing section, and specify the space you want to put between lines in the Between Lines field.

Paragraph Spacing

Within a text box, just pressing the Enter key on your keyboard will begin a new paragraph. What happens though if you wish to add additional white space in between paragraphs? Of course, you are free to repeatedly press the Enter key. Why bother, though, when paragraph spacing can be set?

Click the ≡✎ button in the Paragraph category to add space after a paragraph. From the drop-down option, choose your spacing.

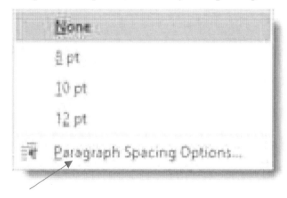

If you want to customize the spacing, click Paragraph Spacing Options.

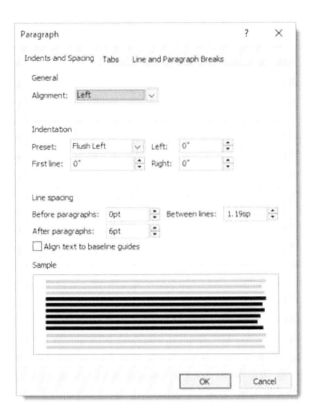

Set the desired amount of space in the Before Paragraphs and After Paragraphs fields under the Line Spacing section.

Indenting Paragraphs

Using these two buttons in the Paragraph group under the Home tab, you may indent paragraphs inside text fields:

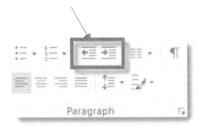

The button on the left decreases in the indention of the paragraph.

The button on the right indents the paragraph.

Setting Tab Stops

Tabs and indents are not nearly the same. You might recall setting the tab stops on your typewriter and using the tab key to accomplish everything from producing bullet points or numbered lists to indenting the opening line of a paragraph. You actually don't require it any longer. The bullet list and numbered list buttons on the word processor make it simple to indent those, and the opening phrase is automatically indented.

If you do need to establish tabs, select the Home tab and then click the arrow to open the box for arranging paragraphs in the lower right corner of the group.

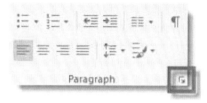

You will then see this dialogue box:

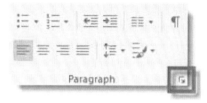

- Click the Tabs tab.

Type a value into the Default tab stops field, then click OK.

Using Styles

Simple character and paragraph properties that you may quickly add to your text are known as styles. Anyone dealing with electronic text is encouraged to utilize styles. They frequently function on several platforms and facilitate the creation of elements like tables of contents.

Additionally, if you alter a style's characteristics, every block of text to which it was applied will be updated to reflect the changes.

Headlines, sub-headlines, body text, sample text, accent text, and other text elements may all be styled.

Go to the Home tab and find the Styles option to add a style to any text. It appears as follows:

Click it to see the available styles or to create your own.

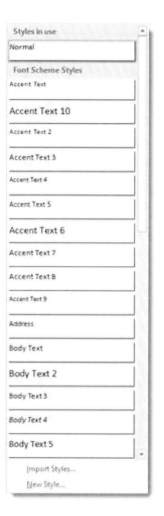

As you can see in the sample above, Publisher comes with a lot of predefined style sets. If you're not happy with those styles, you may import new ones or use those from another software, such MS Word. You will get a popup similar to this when you click New Style:

Here, you may choose the font, character spacing, paragraph structure, and more. You can also give the style a name. When done, click OK.

Click the Style button, then right-click any style, and choose Modify from the menu that appears. Once you've entered your updated settings, click OK.

Correcting Text and Design Errors

You have access to a variety of tools in Publisher to find and fix mistakes in your publication. These may be typographical or design mistakes. We'll demonstrate how to utilize these tools in detail in this portion of the book so that you can maintain your publications uniform and clean and prevent hidden problems from impeding your efforts to have a professional printer reprint them accurately.

Check your Spelling

The majority of our contemporary technology, including iPods, iPads, personal computers, and smart phones, automatically checks our spelling. Publisher is the same. Although it lacks some of the features and sophistication of a specialist word processor like Microsoft Word, it is still more than sufficient. After all, developing publications is Publisher's primary objective. Most likely, you won't write that novel about it.

The Review tab is where you'll discover the spell checking feature, much as in Word. Let's examine it.

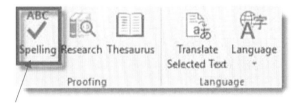

Select the narrative, then click the Spelling icon to verify the spelling. Upon doing so, a dialogue box will open. Keep in mind that in Publisher, a "story" refers to all the content in a single text box or all the material interwoven throughout several text boxes.

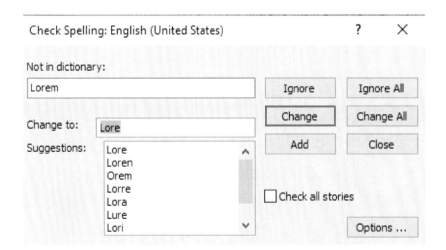

Wherever the pointer is, the procedure starts. The cursor will go from the center of a paragraph in the midst of a tale to the conclusion of the story, then bounce back to the beginning and eventually move back to the point where the cursor was initially placed.

Misspelled words will cause the spell checker to halt while it scans the publication. The dictionary halted on the word "sppedl" in the aforementioned example because it didn't recognize it.

If the word is spelled correctly and you want it to stay that way, you may click the Ignore option to tell Spell Checker to disregard this instance of the term rather than changing the spelling.

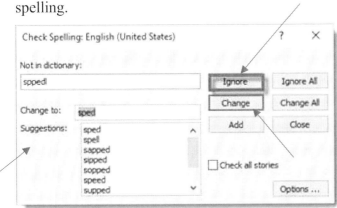

Use the Ignore All button to skip every occurrence of the term in the text of the story.

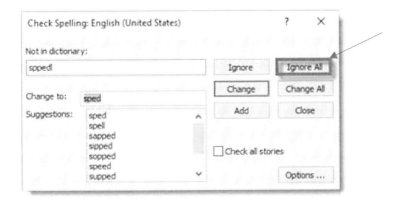

As you can see, Publisher makes an attempt to determine your meaning and automatically inserts what it believes you meant in the Change To box.

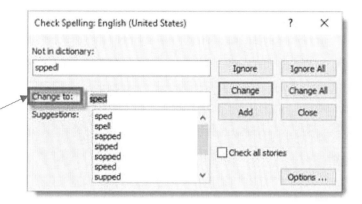

If you click on one of the suggestions, you can choose another word from the list if this one is incorrect.

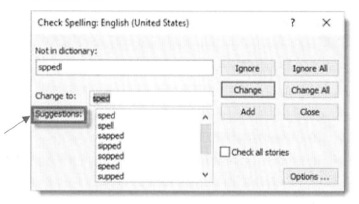

In the Change To box, you may also manually input the precise term. Click the Change button to make the change.

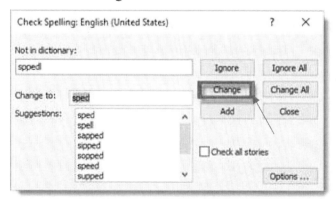

To replace every occurrence of the word with the new word in your publication, use the

Change All option.

To have Spell Checker look over each story in your publication, select the Check all stories option.

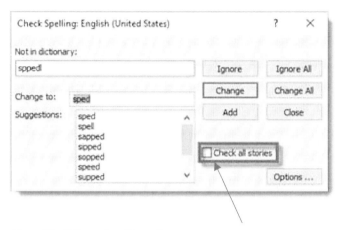

Spell Check Options

To change options in Spell Checker, click Options in the Check Spelling.

Also included is the File tab. Options will appear; click it. Choose Proofing from the left-hand column in the Publisher Options dialogue box.

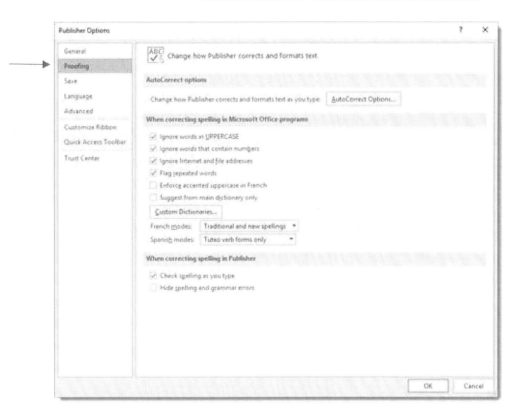

You may opt to omit capital letters, words with numeric characters, internet addresses, etc.

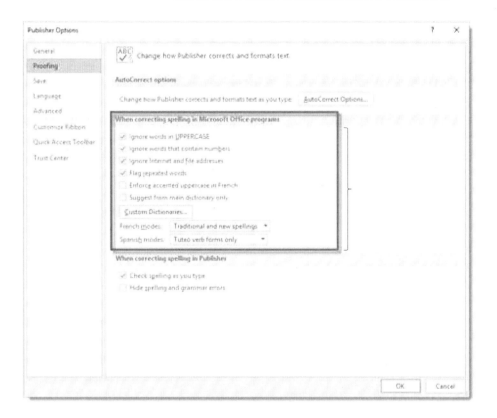

When you select the "Check Spelling As You Type" option, incorrectly spelled words will be

highlighted in red as you type.

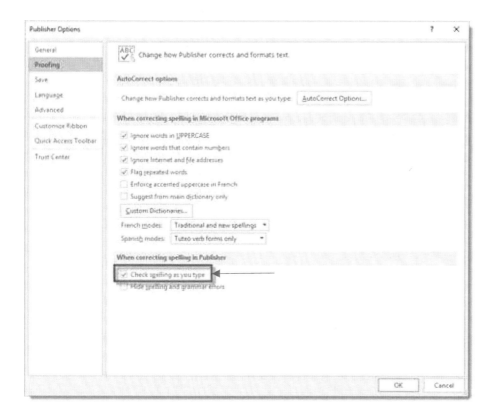

Additionally, you may add terms to your own dictionary to prevent frequently typed words from being flagged as misspelled. To accomplish this, select Custom Dictionaries from the menu.

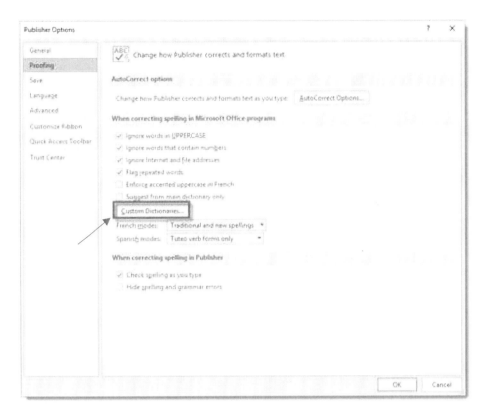

You will then see the Custom Dictionaries dialogue box.

In the Dictionary language drop-down menu, select a language. A new custom dictionary can be added or removed from this page.

Select the dictionary, then click the Modify Word List button to view or edit the terms in any dictionary, even one you've created yourself. This new window will open in a new tab:

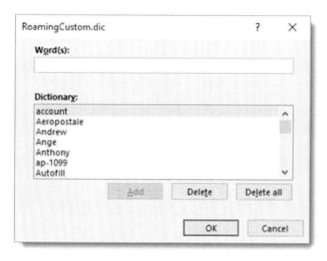

You may use the Word(s) box to search for words, or you can use the Dictionary field and your mouse wheel to navigate through them.

By entering a new term that isn't already in the dictionary and clicking the Add button, you may add words that aren't already in the dictionary.

When done, press OK.

Use AutoCorrect

With the exception of automatically correcting typos and other frequent mistakes, AutoCorrect works in combination with spell checkers. You could, for instance, overlook capitalizing the initial letter of a phrase. Publisher capitalizes it automatically so you don't have to go back and edit it (which would stop you from thinking).

Let's examine some of our possibilities in more detail. Click Options under the File tab to display them. From the left-hand column, select Proofing, then select AutoCorrect Options.

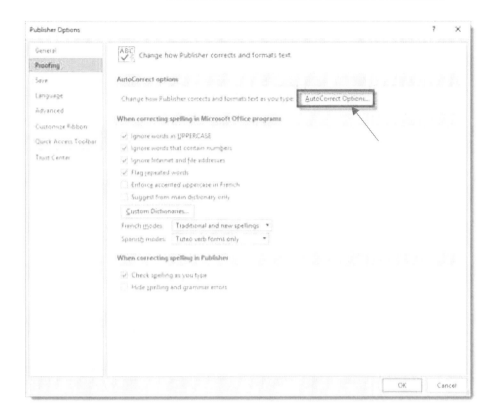

You will then see this dialogue box:

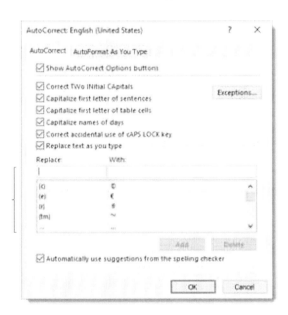

In the example above, you can see how Publisher will change two initial capitals. Actually, touch typists who type really quickly frequently make this mistake. They hold the shift key for a tiny bit longer than necessary. Like we said previously, Publisher may capitalize the initial letter of sentences, table cells, day names, etc.

Now glance at the bottom-left window. Here is a list of keystrokes Publisher will substitute for and what it will do so. For instance, the copyright sign © will be used in lieu of (c). You may also make unique substitutions here.

Publisher occasionally makes unintentional automated corrections. Click the Exceptions button to fix this.

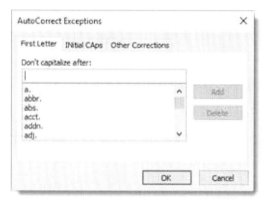

Here you can see stock exceptions and add your own. **Click OK** when finished.

Use Design Checker

Since your magazine already has the style you want, you could be inclined to disregard Design

Checker as a time waster. Simply said, don't. Your publication is not evaluated by Publisher's Design Checker from an aesthetic perspective. It won't suggest, "You have a picture here, and it should go over there to give a feeling of balance," or something like. Or "Your headlines should be in black; they are blue."

Design Checker, on the other hand, flags any mistakes that might prevent your publication from printing correctly.

Go to the File tab and select Info on the left to see the Design Checker button. This is how it seems:

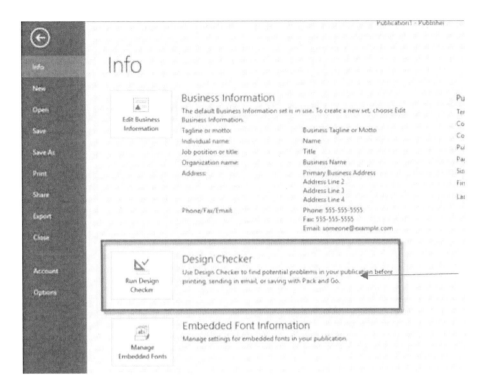

When you press this button, Publisher brings up a window on the right and takes you back to your publication.

Publisher would display any potential faults in our publication here. These things aren't inherently harmful or things that need to be altered. It's possible that you had good reasons for acting in the manner that you did. Publisher is only bringing your attention to any possible mistakes; you are under no obligation to take any action.

To get to the specific error in your publication, click any item displayed in the design checker window.

You can change the parameters by checking boxes at the top of the Design Checker pane. You can ask Publisher to review the overall design, the commercial printing, the website, or the email.

Click the **Design Check Options** link at the bottom of the pane to modify Design Checker settings. There will be a new window.

You may arrange the design concerns from inside this window by description, page number, or status (either fixed or unfixed). Check the Remove Fixed Items box if you only want to view the issues that have not yet been resolved. Additionally, you have the option to include or exclude master pages.

When you choose the Checks tab, a new set of choices appears.

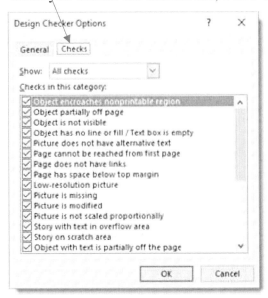

Here, you may specify the possible faults that Publisher should check for. By default, every item is selected, but you can uncheck any of them by clicking on them.

When done, press OK.

Using Undo And Redo

If you find that you have inadvertently deleted, changed or moved text or an object, you can undo the changes that were made and revert to a previous version of the publication. The Undo operation enables you to revert the publication back to the way it was before you made a change, while the Redo operation reverses an Undo operation, redoing the change.

Same File

• Continue using the previous file with this exercise, or open the file Publication Tutorial File_4.pub...

• Ensure that the zoom is set to 100%

• Triple-click in the text above the main heading to select it Press to delete it

• Let's undo the deletion.

• Click on Undo in the Quick Access Toolbar The deleted paragraph will be reinstated.

• Select Information in the main heading, then type Facilities

• Click on Undo in the Quick Access Toolbar; The text will revert back to the original wording...

- Click on Redo in the Quick Access Toolbar; The text will change back to the new wording

To undo previous actions:

- Click on Undo in the Quick Access Toolbar To redo an undone action:

- Click on Redo in the Quick Access Toolbar

- You can use the keyboard shortcut + to quickly undo the previous action.

Alternatively, hold down and press repeatedly to undo consecutive actions.

Saving An Existing Publication

Once a publication has been named and saved for the first time, you can open and close it at will and work in full confidence that, unless it is deleted, it is reasonably safe from computer crashes.

However, you must still save the publication regularly while you are working on it to ensure you do not lose any information you have added since the last time you saved it.

To save an existing document:

- Click on the File tab, then click on Save, or

- Click on Save in the Quick Access Toolbar

- You can use the keyboard shortcut + to quickly save your changes.

Previewing A Publication

The Print place in the Backstage view enables you to view the publication as it would appear on paper before you commit to printing it. The preview is determined by the printer you have selected, so it gives you a more accurate idea of how the publication will print than by viewing it in the design window.

Same File

Continue using the previous file with this exercise, or open the file Publication Tutorial File_6.pub...

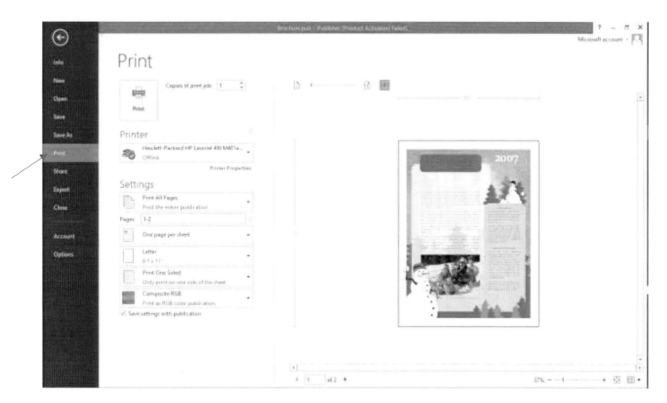

• Click on the File tab, then click on Print. A preview of your publication will be displayed in the right pane, with a range of options to the left...

• Use the Zoom Slider to set the zoom to 100%, as shown

• Click on Fit to Sheet to return to a full page view, as shown

• Click on the drop arrow for Composite RGB in Settings, then select Composite Greyscale. This enables you to see how your publication would appear if printed in black and white.

• Repeat step 4 to return the setting to Composite RGB

• Click on the Back arrow to close the preview

To preview a publication:

- Click on the File tab, then click on Print
- Click on the Back arrow to exit Print Preview

As well as using the File tab to access the printing options in Backstage, you can also press +

Printing A Publication

Traditionally, printing means producing your publication on paper, but in today's web and online world, it might mean printing to the web, printing to another file, or packing the publication ready to be sent to professional printers. Publisher enables you to choose which printer to use, how many copies to make, which pages to print and even to specify special page options.

- Click on the [File tab], then click on Print

The printer options shown will depend on the setup of your particular computer and printer. Notice that there are a range of options available for you to customise your printing process...

- Click on the drop arrow under Printer to see a range of available places to print to.

- Select the desired printer

- Select the desired options under Settings; You can choose to change from the default settings for a range of options, including which pages to print...

- Click on [Print] to print the brochure, or click on the Back arrow to return to the publication without printing

To print a publication:

1. Click on the **[File tab],** then click on [Print]

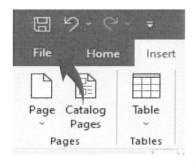

2. Select the appropriate settings

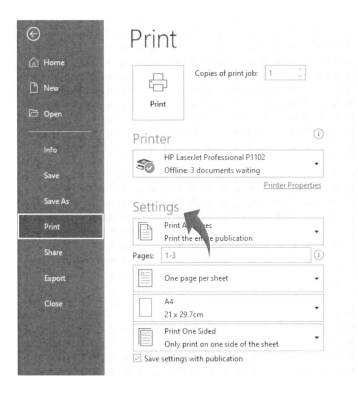

3. Click on [Print]

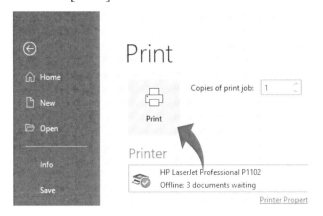

• The options listed under Settings in the middle pane of the Print place in the Backstage will vary depending on the type of publication you are printing.

Safely Closing A Publication

When you create a new publication, a separate Publisher window is opened. To ensure that you do not end up with multiple copies of Publisher open on your computer, you should close the open publication when you have finished with it. When you close a publication you will be prompted to save any changes that you might not have already saved.

Same File

Continue using the previous file with this exercise, or open the file Publication Tutorial File_8.pub...

- Click on the File tab, then click on Close. If you attempt to close a publication that has changed since it was last saved, or if you attempt to close an unsaved publication, a dialog box will appear asking if you want to save the changes.

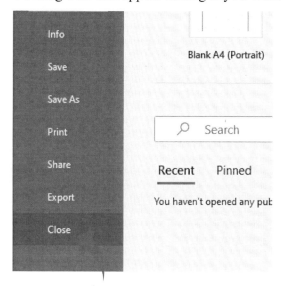

- If a message appears asking if you want to save changes to the publication, click on [Don't Save]. The open publication closes and is replaced by the New options in Backstage view.

To close a publication:

1.   Click on the File tab, then click on Close

2.   If a message appears asking you to save your changes, click on [Save], or Click on [Don't Save]

- If you have more than one publication open, you can swap between them by clicking on the View tab, then clicking on Switch Windows > publication name.

- You can use the keyboard shortcuts + to close a publication.

Chapter 3

Working with a Publication!

In This Chapter

- Knowing & Working on 'The Open Place'
- Using the Open Dialogue Box
- Opening & Working on an Existing Publication
- Using the Pages Navigation Pane
- Inserting & Formatting Pages
- Zooming and Panning
- Moving and Deleting Pages

When you use Publisher to generate a brochure, newsletter, book, or other similar document, you are making a publication. There are core abilities you will need to generate publications successfully, including understanding how to open and work with one that has previously been created. You will learn about:

Learn how to open an existing publication, how to use the Pages navigation pane, how to change the page layout, how to use the zoom and pan on a page, how to insert pages, how to name pages, how to move pages, and how to delete pages, in addition to gaining an understanding of the Open place and how to use the Open dialog box.

The Open Place

The Open Place offers quick access to files that have recently been accessed as well as to storage sites for your data, such as your hard drive or OneDrive. When you use the keyboard shortcut + or click the File tab and select Open, the Open location appears.

The Open Place

The Open location will appear when you visit the Backstage and click on Open (see below for an example). You can open a file you've recently worked on extremely easily because Recent is by default selected in the main pane.

You may access the folders on your computer or in OneDrive by selecting the relevant option in the center pane if the publication you want to open isn't in the list of recently seen publications. When [Browse] is clicked in either location's right pane, the Open dialog box appears, allowing you to go to the appropriate folder and choose which file to open.

By selecting **File > Settings > Advanced > and then in the options box for "Recent Publications,"**

You may modify the number of recent publications that appear in the right pane. Choose a figure between 0 and 50 to display this number of recent publications.

Keyboard Shortcuts

Use the keyboard shortcut + to easily enter the Open location. If you often open and work on the same files or open files that are stored in several locations, you might find this to be helpful.

Using the keyboard shortcut + will take you right to the Open dialog box if you so want.

You may change the settings so that the shortcut + displays the Open dialog box rather of the Open location if you'd want to completely ignore it. If you don't use OneDrive or simply want the Open dialog box to always be shown, this may be helpful. Doing this:

1. To access the Backstage, click the File tab.

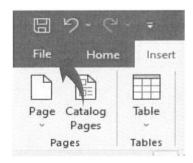

2. To access the Options dialog box, **click Options.**

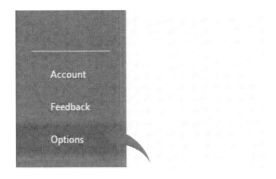

3. In the left pane, **select Save.**

4. Under Save documents, choose **Don't show the Backstage while opening or saving files.**

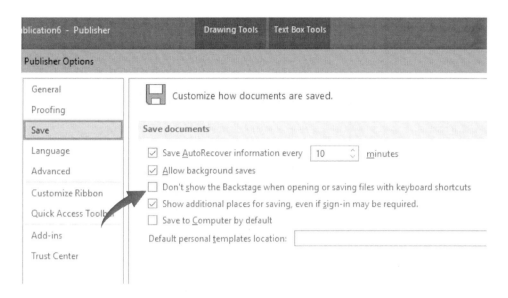

5.   Select [OK].

Note: By choosing this option, the Backstage will not show up when you use the shortcut to save your work; instead, the Save As dialog box will open automatically.

Additionally, keep in mind that changing this setting in Publisher or any Office software will affect all Office products.

The Open Dialog Box

You need to show the Open location in the Backstage and open the Open dialog box in order to access publications that have previously been written and saved on your computer, network, or other storage device (other than OneDrive). The following provides an explanation of the choices available in the Open dialog box for files saved to your computer.

The Open Dialog Box Options

1.   The folders and subfolders that are contained inside the listed storage devices are shown in the Navigation pane. This pane is divided into two sections: a list of Favorites in the upper half and a list of all Folders in the below. To find the necessary publication, utilize the Navigation window to navigate through the various directories and subfolders. To reveal and hide the hierarchy inside folders, click the arrows to expand and collapse the folders. To view a folder's contents in the File List window, click on its name.

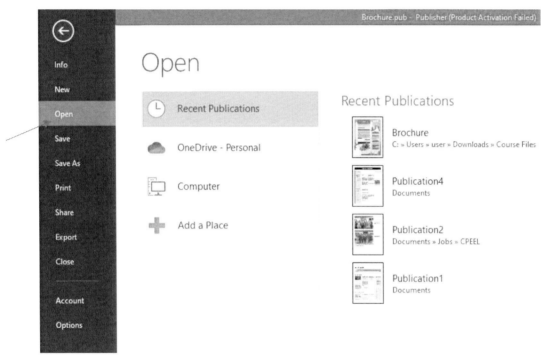

•   You may manage how the files displayed in the dialog box are organized and presented using the toolbar buttons.

•   For instance, you may modify the File List to display the files as icons rather than a list using the Change your view tool or move and rename files with the Organize tool.

•   The folders you select when you click on one in the Navigation pane are saved in the background. You can go back through previously visited folders using the Back button, and you can go ahead through them once again with the Forward button.

• The File List pane's presently visible files' file path locations are shown in the Address Bar.

• You may find a file by using search parameters in the search box. For more sophisticated searches, these criteria may include Boolean operators (like AND, NOT, OR, etc.) and be based on the file name, file type, or author.

• The files and subfolders included in the folder that is presently chosen in the Navigation pane are listed in the File List pane. To open a folder or file from this list, double-click on it. There are several options in this section near the bottom of the dialog box. The name of the selected file is displayed in the File name box. To see a list of recently opened files, click the drop arrow next to the File name.

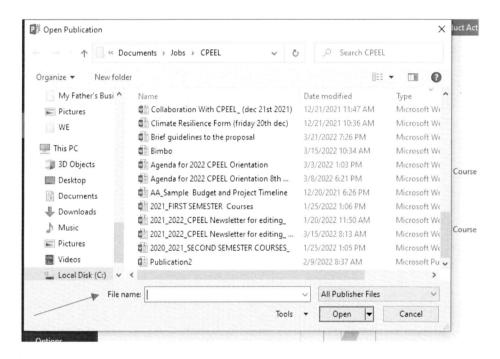

Additional tools for the dialog box are shown under the Tools option. To open the file shown in File name, click [Open], or to dismiss the dialog box without opening a file, click [Cancel].

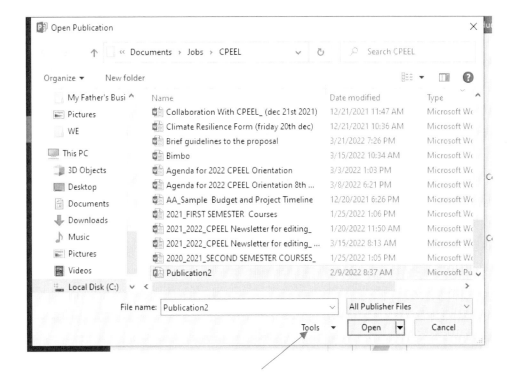

Opening An Existing Publication

One may open an existing publication in a variety of methods, including by double-clicking a file in File Explorer or by right-clicking the Publisher shortcut on the desktop taskbar and choosing a publication from the Recent list. But if Publisher is already open, selecting Open from the Backstage menu is the simplest way to access an existing publication.

Be sure Publisher has launched before beginning this activity.

- To see the Backstage, select the File tab. Then, click Open to see a list of sites where you may open files. The default selection will be recent publications...

- The Open dialog box will appear once you click Browse after clicking This PC in the main pane.

Double-click the Local Disk (C:) disk located in the Navigation pane's This PC section. The file list will show the contents of the C: disk.

To view its contents, double-click on Course Files for Microsoft Publisher 2016. The files for this course are placed in this folder.

• Click Working With A Publication_ once you scroll there. 1.pub and choose [Open] to view it

To access an already published work:

1. Select the File tab and then select Open.

2. After choosing the necessary place, select [Browse].

• To display the Open location in the Backstage, press the + keyboard shortcut.

• To open a publication you've used lately, choose your file from the Recent Publications list after clicking Recent in the Backstage menu, then click Open.

3. Select the necessary file.

4. Select [Open].

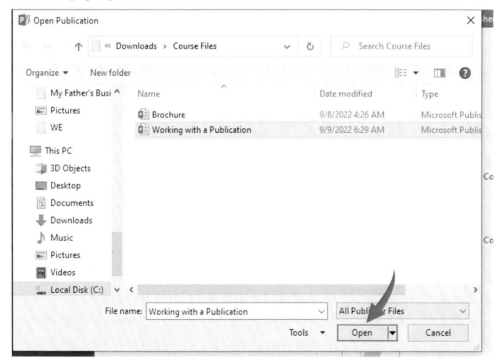

Using The Pages Navigation Pane

You could work on or produce publications that have numerous pages. For instance, you may produce a multi-page brochure or a pricing list that lists every good and service your business provides. You may navigate between the publication's pages by using the Pages navigation window on the left side of the screen.

Changing pages involves:

- In the Pages navigation box, click the desired page to visit it.
- Click on the arrow at the top of the Pages navigation pane to collapse or enlarge the window.

- By utilizing the Go To Page dialog box, you may travel to a certain page. Selecting Go To Page

- from the drop-down menu for Find in the Editing group on the Home tab will bring up this dialog

- box. In a book with many pages, this option could be helpful.

Working With Layouts

When you first open a new publication, it will by default be seen in Normal mode with a Single Page layout. Two-Page Spread is the alternate layout that may be used in Normal view to display two adjacent pages of the document side by side. Both the status bar and the View tab provide these layout choices.

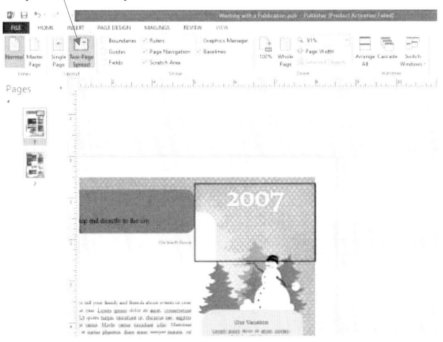

- In the Layout group, select Single Page. Take note of the modified thumbnail previews in the Pages navigation window.

- Click on page 2 in the Pages navigation pane

There is another way to change the layout of a publication…

•   As shown, click on Two-Page Spread in the status bar.

To alter the design of a publication:

1) Select the View tab.

2. Select the right choice from the Layout group by clicking.

•   By right-clicking a page in the Pages navigation pane and choosing the corresponding item from the shortcut menu, you may change between a single page and a two-page spread.

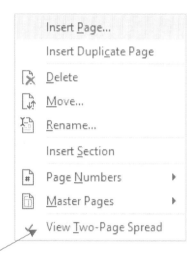

Zooming And Panning

You might occasionally wish to zoom in on a particular section of a publication. This stage can be completed by panning and zooming. With the help of the zoom tools, you may enlarge or reduce the size of a publication, and the scroll bars let you move the active page up, down, to the left, or to the right.

Make sure the publication's second and third pages are visible, then select the View tab.
Select 100% from the Zoom group.

The text in the publication will be 100% enlarged. Let's get even closer now.

• Select 200% by selecting the drop-down arrow next to Zoom on the View tab.

The publication will be 200% enlarged. Let's zoom in on a page corner. Until the top of the page is displayed, hold down the mouse button or continually click the arrow on the side scroll bar. Until the top corner of the page is visible, hold down the mouse button or continually click the arrow to the left of the bottom scroll bar. Let's restore full page visibility. To fit the page to the display area, click Whole Page in the Zoom group on the View tab.

When you want to change the zoom level on a page, click the View tab, then the drop-down arrow next to Zoom in the Zoom group.

• Click and drag the scroll bars until the page is in the correct place to pan across or up and down a page.

• You may pan up and down the displayed page as well as zoom in and out using the mouse wheel.

Simply use the mouse wheel to navigate backwards or forwards to pan up and down a page. Hold down while moving the mouse wheel backwards or forwards to zoom in or out.

Inserting Pages

You'll undoubtedly need to include pages into your publications at some point. For instance, if you need to create a huge publication, the pages included in the template may not be large enough to accommodate the material, or you may wish to create a publication that is completely blank and has a certain number of pages. Fortunately, you may add more pages to a publication at any time.

Inserting pages:

1. From the Pages group, choose the bottom half of the page by clicking on the Insert tab.

2. To open the Insert Page dialog box, choose Insert Page.

3. Choose the choices as necessary, then choose [OK].

• You have three options when adding a new page: a blank one, one with a text field, or a copy of the currently chosen page.

Naming Pages

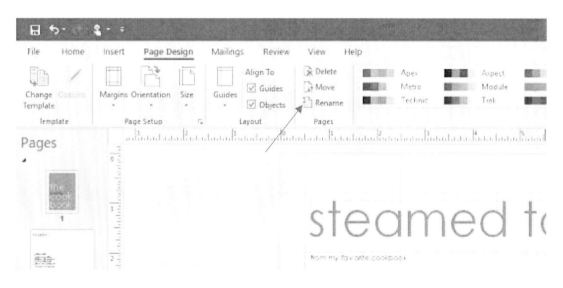

Figure: name changing of pages

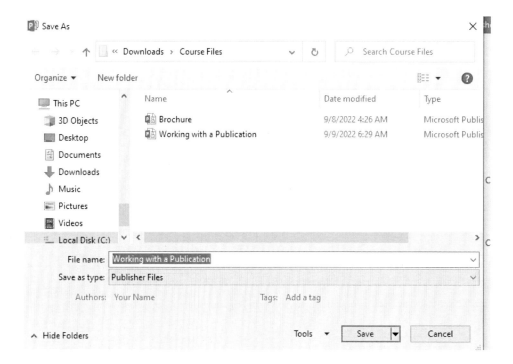

Working with a sizable magazine makes it challenging to keep track of the contents of each page.

This is particularly true if each page can only be identified by its number. Fortunately, Publisher lets you give pages names to make them simpler to recognize.

Renaming a page:

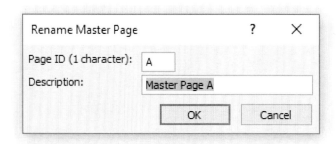

1.   In the Pages navigation pane, select the page to be renamed.

2.   Next, select the Page Design tab

3.   Within the Pages section, select Rename. After entering the new page's name, click [OK].

•   Dividing your pages into parts may be helpful if you have a lot of them. Simply pick Insert Section from the context menu by right-clicking a page in the Pages navigation pane. You may move pages between parts as needed and expand or collapse sections to view or conceal them.

Moving Pages

Making a publication requires creativity, so you'll definitely need to make adjustments as you go.

You could discover, for instance, that a different sequence for the pages you've produced might be more effective. Fortunately, adjusting a publication's page order is a quick and simple operation.

Open the file Working With A Publication 6.pub to continue with the preceding file's exercise.

Click pages 2 and 3 to choose them in the Pages navigation window. To view the Move Page dialog box, select the Page Design tab, then click Move in the Pages group.

Make sure After is selected under Move selected pages after making sure Both pages are selected under Which page. Click Page 5 in this page. Lunch as shown To place the chosen pages after the Lunch page, click [OK].

Pages 4 and 5 of the publication are created from the pages.

Changing the page:

1. In the Pages navigation pane, choose the page you want to relocate, then select the Page Design option.

2. Select Move under the Pages section.

3. Click [OK] after selecting the required choices in the Move Page dialog box.

- Right-clicking the page you want to move and choosing Move will bring up the Move Page dialog box.

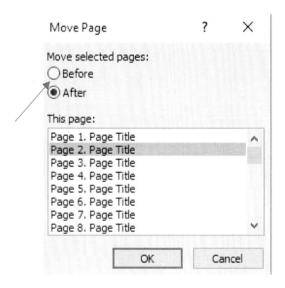

Figure: Showing how to move pages before and after a certain page

In the Pages navigation pane, you may reposition pages by clicking and dragging them to the desired location.

Deleting Pages

It's possible that when making publications with several pages, some of the pages won't be needed.

This may happen if you included more blank pages than you actually needed or if the material on some of the pages started to go out-of-date. Fortunately, Publisher makes it simple and quick to delete pages.

Open the file Working With A Publication 7.pub to continue with the preceding file's exercise.

• In the Pages navigation window, choose pages 4 and 5. The Delete Page dialog box will appear after selecting the Page Design tab and clicking Delete in the Pages group.

To remove the pages, make sure Both pages are selected and then click [OK]. Getting rid of a page

1. In the Pages navigation pane, click the page you want to remove.

2. In the Pages group, click Delete after selecting the Page Design tab.

• If you've added, removed, or moved pages, page numbers will immediately update in your publication to reflect the changes.

• To delete a page, use a right-click in the Pages navigation bar and choose Delete.

Chapter 4

Working with Text!

In This Chapter

- Creating a Text Box
- Modifying a Text Box
- Importing Text Box
- Checking Spelling
- Inserting & Formatting Text
- Applying Color to Text
- Creating and Formatting WordArt

INFOCUS

Publisher offers several options for improving the appearance of your publication, including text enhancement tools. Once you understand how to enter text, you can change the font, color, size, WordArt features, and choose from a variety of typography options and other effects. All of these alternatives will help make certain pieces of text stand out more than others, but use them sparingly so your post doesn't look cluttered and cluttered.

In this chapter, you'll learn how to import text, edit text boxes, spell check publications, create text boxes, customize text boxes, and select text.

- Learn how to create WordArt;
- How to format WordArt;
- How to add text effects;
- How to add color to text.

Creating A Text Box

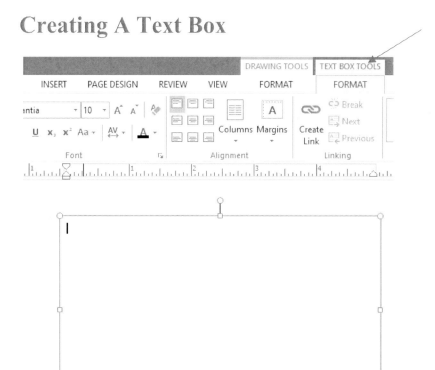

Figure: Creating a textbox

An object used to hold text in a text box.

You can resize, move, group, arrange and format like any other object. Another unique feature of text boxes is that you can control the behavior of the text. For example, you can change the border between text and frames, wrap text around objects, merge text frames, and create columns. Before starting this walkthrough, you need to open the Working with Text 1.pub file.

- Select the Home tab and click the Insert Text Box button under the Objects group. A cross appears instead of the mouse pointer.
- Click and drag below the Greetings heading to create a hint text box. • When a text box is selected, its border is displayed as a solid line.
- Select a text box by clicking anywhere on the page. It seems to disappear.

- Show Text Box: The border of the text box appears as a dotted line and the mouse cursor changes shape to indicate that it is not currently selected..

Making a text box:

1. Click the Draw Text Box button under the Objects group on the Home tab.

2. To draw a text box, position the mouse and then click and drag.

3. Click the mouse button to stop.

• Hold down when drawing a text box if you want it to be square.

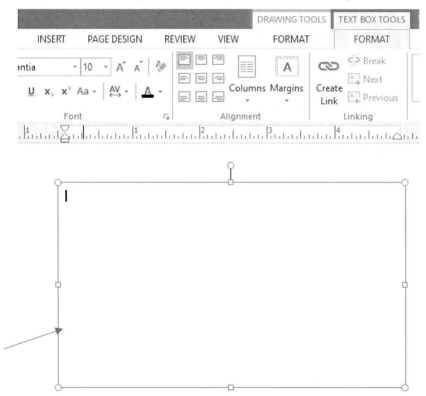

Figure: A Square Text Box

Modifying A Text Box

As with most creative processes, you can always make small adjustments to your publication. Includes adjustments for text boxes. I doubt that every text field you create is exactly what you need. Fortunately, text boxes can be easily resized, and Publisher makes it easy to align them with other elements on the page. Open the file or use the previous file to continue this operation. Enable Text Click the text box below the Welcome title on the publication's home page to enable it. Mouse over the square size handle at the bottom of the text box to create a double-headed arrow.

Press and hold the handle until the pink guides appear, drag down and release the mouse button as shown.

- Repeat steps 2, 3, and 4 for the square size handle on the right edge of the text box, then click and drag the handle toward the right edge of the page to enlarge the text box as shown..

To change a text box's size:

1. Select the edge you want to move and click the sizing handle.
2. Click and drag the sizing handles to resize the text box.

• You can change the length and width of a text box at the same time by clicking and dragging one of the round sizing handles in the corners of the border.

• As you move or resize objects, pink guides appear to help you align them with other objects on the page.

Importing Text

Publisher lets you import text from other sources, such as word processing programs, or enter text directly into text fields. Imported text is automatically formatted using Publisher's general style settings. To protect the formatting, if you prepare the text before importing (eg in Microsoft Word), you must set the style in Word and apply it to the text.

To continue with this walkthrough, open Working with Text 3.pub or use the previous file. Make sure the text box under the Greetings heading is checked. To open the Insert Text dialog box, click the Insert tab, and then in the Text group, click Insert File. After opening the Course Files folder, find and click on the Newsletter Text 1.docx file.

- Click OK to add the text from the file to your publication. After converting to Publisher format, the text is entered into the text field..

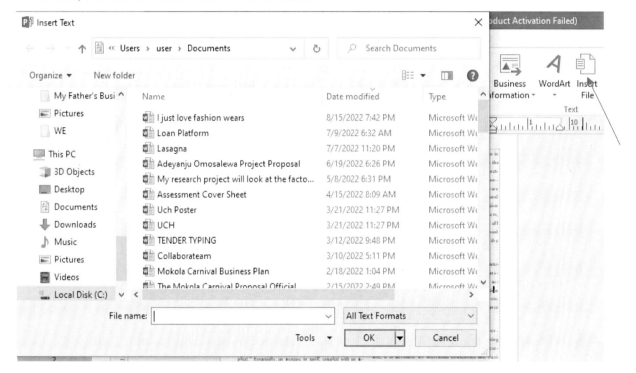

Adding text to a publication involves:

1. Select the text box where the imported text will be by clicking.

2. In the Text group, choose Insert File from the Insert menu.

3. Select [OK] after finding the file the imported text will come from.

• Publisher will insert some of the imported text in the designated text box if it doesn't fit completely, then build a new text box on a new page to accommodate the extra content. If you want to fit all of the content in one text box, you might have to play with the text layout.

Checking Spelling

The Microsoft Office spell check feature is used by Publisher. Spell checking analyzes your writing, looks for misspellings and redundant terms, and then suggests modifications. Be careful that because they don't appear in the dictionary, spell check frequently pauses on less popular terms and names that are spelled correctly.

Same File

Open Working with Text 4.pub to continue using the old file for this walkthrough. Click the first line of the text box under the Greetings heading, select the Check tab, and in the Spelling group, open the Check Spelling dialog box. May indicate correctly prescribed diarrhea.

If necessary, select Ignore to ignore and display the next possible problem. Sorry

Click Change to accept the highlighted offer. After you have selected the correct proposal from the proposal, click Change to change the annual spelling. To select all text boxes in your Publisher publication, click the Check all items check box until a check box appears. Click [Edit] to edit the conversation. You will be prompted to read the rest of the post.

• For further questions, choose Yes and then Ignore.

You will be notified when the spell check is complete. Click OK to return to publishing.

Spelling accuracy:

1. Select Spelling from the Spell Check category on the Browse menu.

2. Click [Change], [Add] or [Ignore] as required.

3. Choose Yes to select additional text boxes.

4. Choose OK.

• When the spell checker stops at the wrong generic term, click Add. Future spell checkers will ignore the term and add it to the dictionary.

• If a name is spelled correctly but appears more than once, select Ignore All to skip these instances.

Selecting Text

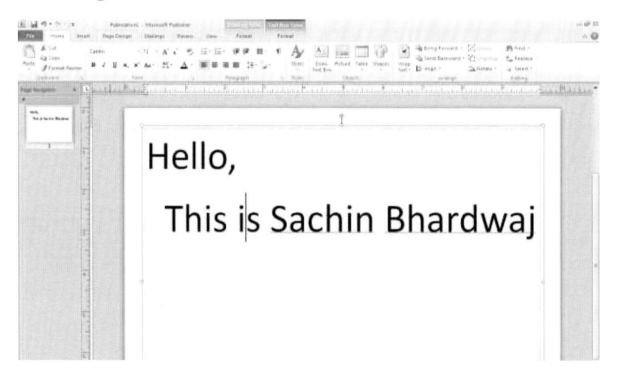

Figure: Selecting a Text in Publisher

Before making changes, you must select the text of the post you want to change.

There are several methods, depending on how much text you need to select and where you need to move it from. Each selection method can be used at different times.

- Open the file or use the previous file to continue this operation. 5.Use ad text... You need to click on the first word of the text after the greeting title. Click and drag to the end of the second paragraph of text, then release the mouse button.

- The first two sentences of the text are selected. To deselect, click outside the text, then click again on the first word of the text.

- Click and hold when you click the end of the third paragraph of text. The first three sentences of the text are selected.

- Click outside the text to remove it. Then click anywhere in the text box.

- Click the + button to select all the text in the text field.

To choose text:

1. Select the text by clicking at the beginning.

2. Click and drag the cursor to the end of the desired text or

• If the text box contains text that is not visible (that is, text that "floats" because it does not fit in the field), it is very useful to use the + method to select all the text and click at the end of the text. . Invisible and visible text are selected along with visible text.

Applying Color To Text

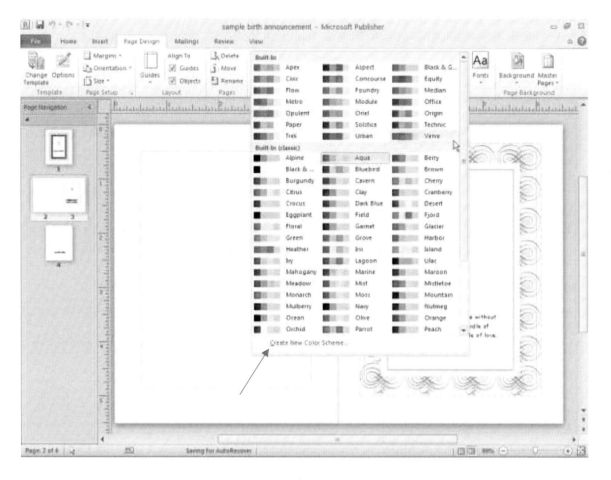

You can use color to make the text stand out. The color scheme of an ad can convey a certain mood or brand identity of a company. The active color scheme determines the initial color selection.

This ensures quick creation of color matching magazines. You can also skip the color scheme and choose a different color.

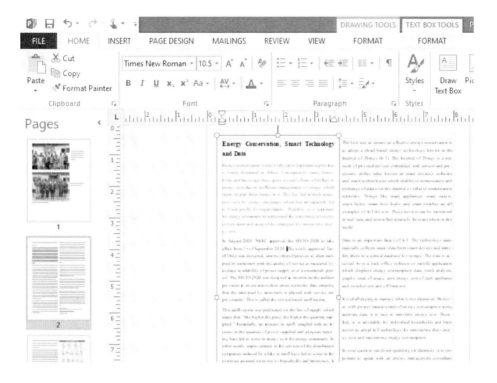

Figure: Changing the color of a text.

1. Select text.
2. Click the drop-down arrow next to Font to select additional colors to open the Colors dialog box. The color in the Font group on the Home tab.
3. Select the desired color and click [OK]. You can access the color wheel from the Custom tab of the Color dialog box. This allows you to select a specific color instead of a color from the palette on the main page.

Creating WordArt

WordArt is decorative text, usually preformatted with color, borders, shadows, fonts, and initial word shapes. Choose a design from your WordArt library and enter the words you want to create WordArt for. The editor will format the text you provide with the design you choose.

Creating WordArt

1. Click the Insert tab and select WordArt in the Text group.

2. Select Design to display the Edit WordArt Text dialog box.

3. Enter the desired text and click [OK].

• WordArt can be created from existing text.

First select the text and then enter the word editing dialog. The selected text appears in the text box of the dialog box.

Figure: Editing WordArt Text

Formatting WordArt

WordArt, like any other object in Publisher, offers many options for formatting text. This WordArt format consists of effects and paint colors that you can add or change using dialog boxes. You can completely change the layout or make minor adjustments to the layout of your magazine.

1. Select the WordArt file you want to format.

2. WordArt Tools: Select the Format tab, then select Dialog Launcher in the WordArt Styles group.

3. After making any necessary changes, click [OK].

• To format, right-click the WordArt and choose Format WordArt to open the Format WordArt dialog box.

Text Effects

You can use Publisher's tools to add a variety of effects to the text in your publication. These can be lighting effects, shadows, and basic fill effects such as underlining and capitalization. Be careful when using these effects, as they can make your posts look weird or hard to read.

To render a text effect:

One. To display the Fonts dialog box, select the text, click the Home tab, and then click the Font Groups dialog box launcher.

2. Click the Fill Effect button to open the Format Text Effect dialog box.

3. After setting the appropriate effect, click [OK].

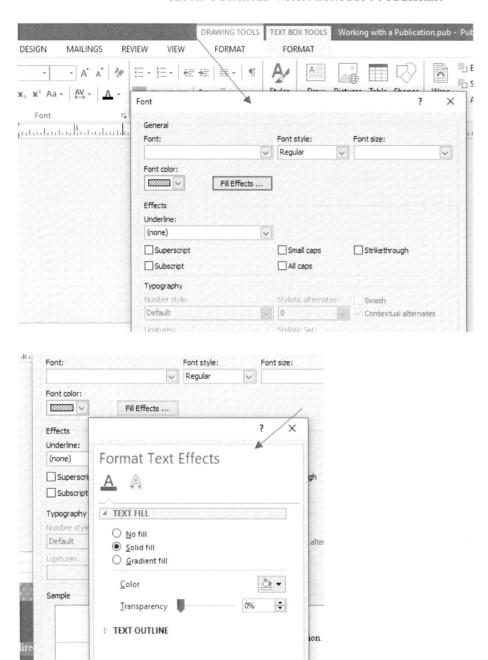

Figure: Fill Effects Dialog

• Typography settings let you change things like ligatures and underlining, and add effects like capitalization to the text in your publication. You can also choose from stylish alternatives to a variety of fonts. Text Box Tools: More options are available on the Format tab..

Today I Learned in this chapter (A Little Game):

List all what you have learnt in this chapter and the most important piece of information that you never knew you needed in this chapter.

Chapter 5

Text Techniques!

In This Chapter

- Using Text Columns & Linking Text Boxes
- Drawing Text Box Accurately
- Aligning Text Using Baseline Guides
- Paragraph Spacing & Hyphenation
- Creating Bulleted Lists & Numbered Lists
- Creating & Applying Text Style
- Understanding the Layout Guides Dialogue Box in Publisher

INFOCUS

You might need to sometimes alter the way the text is laid up in your magazine. For instance, you could wish to arrange an article for a newsletter as columns or to have the content begin on one page and end on another. You may easily produce publications that are consistent and appear professional by using options like these (and many more).

You will:

- find out how to make text columns
- discover how to connect text boxes
- develop your ability to precisely create text boxes
- discover how to alter text box borders
- get to know text wrapping
- become knowledgeable about text-box alignment
- become familiar with baseline standards for text alignment
- become familiar with paragraph spacing
- learn how to apply text styles;

- learn how to create bulleted lists;
- learn how to create numbered lists;
- learn how to set hyphenation;
- learn how to make lists with headings;
- learn how to create lists with bullets.

Text Columns

You may want text to include columns in publications such as newsletters and flyers. This can be done by changing the properties (or properties) of the text box. You can use the properties to set the width between the text box columns and the desired number of columns in the text box.

Add a column to the text box like this:

1. Click in the text box.

2. Select the Text Box tool. Select additional columns by selecting the Format tab drop-down arrow next to the column header in the Sort group.

3. Change the settings if necessary.

• Click the "Columns" button to easily select multiple columns from the menu. However, the default distance is used.

• The text box tools and column options are all on the Home tab..

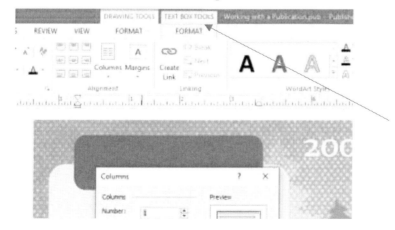

Figure: Text Box Tools and Columns

Linking Text Boxes

You can add text boxes in Publisher so that text flows from one text box to another. To grab the reader's attention, you can start your story on the front page of a newspaper and continue on another page. Even if you change the plot, the editor rearranges (redistributes) the text between bars.

To continue the exercise from the previous file, open Text Techniques 2.pub.

- To enter text, select the text field next to the "Visit Dream Cultural Center" heading. As you can see, the handle is red, not white. This indicates that there is more content than can fit in this text area.

Text Box Tools: On the Format tab, in the Links group, click Create Link. The jar icon appears with the mouse pointer.

- To view the second and third pages of the document, click Pages 2 and 3 in the page navigation bar. See the section under the heading on page 2. As seen in the image, the dream goes to the cultural center (continued). Here the text field is empty.
- Connect the text box to the main page text box by making the mouse pointer a jar. Then click the text box to add the text that doesn't fit into the first text box.

Connecting text boxes

1. Select the top text box.

2. In the Linking group, select Create Link under the Text Box Tools: Format tab.

3. Press the second text box by clicking.

• A little square with a black arrow on it appears on the edge of the connected text field when it is chosen. The text box to which this box is attached will become active if you click on the arrow.

146

Drawing Text Boxes Accurately

Draw text boxes without worrying about size or position. However, there are situations where perfect text alignment is required, such as when using pre-printed forms. When you create a text box, you can use the page coordinates and drawing dimensions displayed in the status bar as a template.

To continue this explanation, open Text Techniques 3.pub or use the previous file. In the Page Navigation pane, select Page 1, and then on the Home tab, in the Objects group, choose Draw Text Box. Display the text just above the word Host and to the left below the title "The Dream Comes to the Cultural Center" as shown. Let's create a text box of a certain size using the status bar.

Focus on the status bar and click and drag while tracking the status bar to create a text box until the status bar is about 1.5" X 1.5".

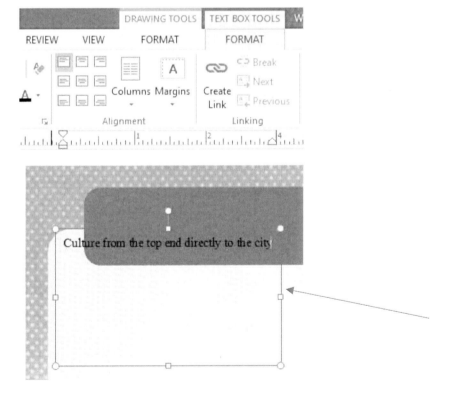

Figure: Creating a text box

Release the mouse button to create a text box. Enter "... culture straight from the rooftop to the city." After selecting the text, go to the Home tab, in the Font group, click the drop-down arrow, scroll down and select Times New Roman. • For a more detailed view of the changes, go elsewhere in the publication.

• To create an exact text box:

1. On the Home tab, in the Objects group, click the Draw Text Box button.

2. Resize the text box to the desired size while viewing the dimensions in the status bar.

• In the Format Text Box dialog box, you can change the size and position of the text box after drawing. With the text box selected, display this dialog box by clicking Text Box Tools: Format tab, and then clicking the Text Groups dialog box launcher.

Text Box Margins

Figure: Text Box Margins

The appropriate use of white space is a key strategy in designing an effective layout for your publications. The unprinted space between lines and text blocks is known as white space. Numerous studies have demonstrated that a message is easier for the human eye to read and understand when it is surrounded by white space. Increasing the text box's internal margins is one technique to do this.

Margin changes for text boxes:0

1. Click to select the text box. Click on the text group dialog launcher below.

Tools: Format tab.

2. Enter the desired margins for the top, bottom, left, and right and click [OK].

• Use auto-fit settings to prevent "overfilling" of text boxes. Click the text box, click Text Box Tools: Format tab, and in the Text group, click Align Text to see options. If you hover, a tooltip appears that explains what each option does.

Wrapping Text

You can force the text in a text box to wrap around text cells and other elements on the page. Text boxes encapsulate text when placed in front of other elements. As a result, front text boxes take precedence over back text boxes, so changing the layer or order of text boxes on the page can change how the text fits.

To continue this explanation, open Text Techniques 5.pub or use the previous file. To view the pages, click on pages 2 and 3 in the page navigation bar. On page 2, click on the text box next to the title "Dream of the Cultural Center". (continuation)

- To open the Format Text Box dialog box, click Drawing Tools: Format tab, click Wrap Text in the Adjustments group, and then click More Layout Options. Text forces each preceding element to wrap on both sides using the current wrap settings.
- You can close the dialog box by choosing Cancel.

Select the Home tab, Draw Text Box and Objects to draw a small text box as shown below. Wrap the text in the larger text box to make room for the new text box.

- A didgeridoo performance takes place during the performances. Move the mouse away from the text box to clearly see the changes.

To set text wrapping for a text box:

1. First select the text box.

2. Drawing Tools: On the Format tab, under Text Wrap, in the Adjustment group, click Advanced Layout Options.

3. Choose a package option and choose OK.

• Each text wrapping option has a slightly different effect on your publication. For example, the Top and Bottom options split the text around the element on its own path, while the Close option makes the text flow as close to the object as possible..

Aligning Text

In addition to aligning elements on the page, you can align text in text boxes. You can inline each paragraph. This means that text can be spaced to fill the entire space on each line, or justified to the left, center, or right of a specified area. You will find yourself using different types of alignment when publishing.

To continue with this exercise, open the Text Techniques 6.pub file or use the file you used previously. In the page navigation pane, select page 1, then select the first sentence of the text below the opening heading. By default, paragraphs are on the left. To see how the text aligns to the right of the column, on the Home tab, in the Paragraph group, click Align Right. Let's change the general direction of the article. After you have selected all the text in the text box, click the Arrange button in the Paragraph group.

This is a path often used in newspapers and other publications.

Repeat step 3 to apply justification to the second item on the page. It is emblazoned with the words "...a culture that goes straight from the hills to the city."

Let's adjust the direction of the text inside this text box. To align the text, select the Text Box tool and choose Align Center from the Alignment group.

Format tab.

Text alignment:

1. To align a paragraph, click within it or choose the text to align.

2. Select the Home tab, then under the Paragraph group, select the appropriate alignment choice.

• The Text Box Tools: Format tab offers options for both vertical and horizontal text alignment. When working with text boxes that have a limited quantity of text in them, you might find this helpful.

Using Baseline Guides

Text can be aligned using baseline guides to create a uniform appearance across columns. Baseline guides guarantee that text is uniformly spaced down a column and that each line is aligned with a matching line in the adjacent column by showing a design grid.

Baseline guidelines are a component of Microsoft Publisher's collection of layout instructions.

For baseline guidance and text alignment:

1. Choose the text.

2. Select the Home tab, then pick the Launcher for the Dialog Box for the Paragraph group.

3. Tick the box next to Align text to baseline guidelines.

4. Select [OK].

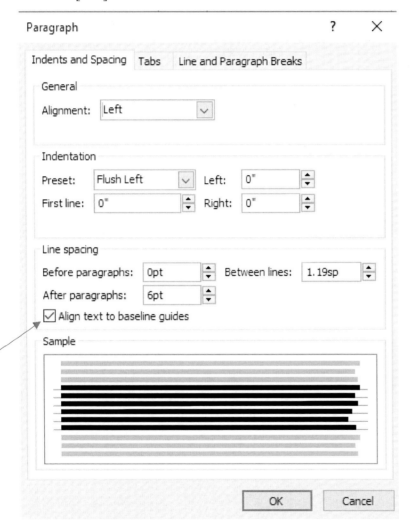

Figure: Check Box for aligning text to baseline guides

To show or conceal baseline guides:

1) Select the View tab.

2. Tick or Un-tick Baselines by clicking on it.

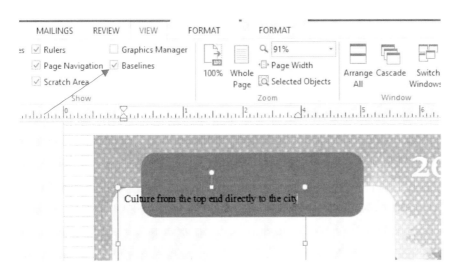

Figure: Ticking and Unticking Baselines

Paragraph Spacing

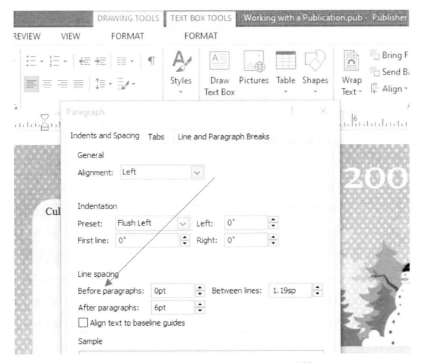

Figure: Paragraph Spacing between each line of the paragraph

You can adjust paragraph and line spacing using the Paragraph settings in Publisher. You can specify specific spacing before, after, and/or between each line in a paragraph. Paragraph breaks can make paragraphs easier to separate and make content easier to read.

To continue this exercise, open Text Techniques 8.pub or use the file you used previously. The welcome section on the main page of the publication should be fully selected. To view the Paragraph dialog box, select the Home tab and click the Paragraph Group dialog box launcher. Adjust the line spacing by clicking the down arrow on the spinner until you reach 0pt after the paragraph. show.

- After you click OK, click anywhere else on the page to remove spaces between paragraphs of text, making it easier to see your changes. The text is harder to read.
- Repeat steps 1 and 2 to select the text and return to the Paragraph dialog box.
- Click the up arrow on the spinner until Line Spacing after Paragraph is set to 5 pt. Click OK to adjust the spacing after each paragraph to 5 pt, then click elsewhere on the page to clearly see the change.

How to adjust paragraph spacing

1. Select text.

2. Select the Home tab and select the Run dialog for the Paragraph group.

3. After setting the front, back and between lines of the line, click [OK].

• If Paragraph Spacing is set to a value greater than 0, the first paragraph will have a space. When the text is formatted as a column, the top of the first column does not fit into the other columns and the problem occurs.

Hyphenation

If you type a big word that doesn't match at all, the term is automatically broken. We call this a dash. You can remove extra dashes by turning off automatic dash. In addition to the manual hyphenation option, which gives you the option to break long words, you can also hyphenate manually. On the first page of the publication, select All Content in the Getting Started section. You will notice that there is a hyphen that separates certain words into two lines.

- To open the Hyphenation dialog box, select Hyphen in the Text group under Text Box Tools: Format tab.

- Click this event to display an automatic dash with no checkmark.

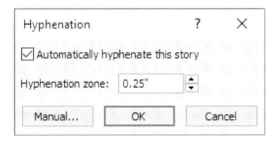

• To view text without hyphens, click the [OK] button and then click anywhere on the page. The text may not fit in the current text box.

• Repeat steps 1-4 to reactivate Auto Stop.

Removing the hyphenation

1. Press the text box.

2. Select Hyphenation from the Text group under the Text Box Tools: Format tab.

3. Uncheck the box next to Automatically hyphenate this article.

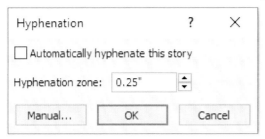

• By selecting [Manual] from the Hyphenation dialog box, you can opt to manually choose which words to hyphenate. For each word that was automatically hyphenated in the chosen text field, you will be given the option to pick [Yes] or [No].

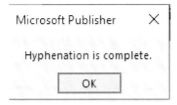

Creating Bulleted Lists

Placing a symbol or other special character at the beginning of a sentence or line of text constitutes punctuation. You can use many symbols, but the most basic symbol for Microsoft Office products is a filled circle. Item lists use bullet points to make them easier to recognize and read. Bulleted lists are used when there is no clear hierarchy or importance between the items in the list. Click on the front page of the magazine after the paragraph in the What to Expect While Dreaming text box.

Click to display a list of options, and then on the Home tab, in the Paragraph group, choose Characters. Enter live dance performances and didgeridoos, then select Small Bullets (first option) and click on the bullet list to begin.

The next line will automatically receive a new token. After each item is displayed, tap to see a list. You may need to move the bottom edge of the text box down to make it a little bigger. Click the extra marker at the end of the list to remove it, then click the text box in the text box to delete the text.

To start a bulleted list:

1. Click to start a new line.

2. In the Paragraph group, on the Home tab, choose Character.

Almost any symbol can be used as a symbol. Just select Type to open the Symbols dialog box, click Type to open the Symbols and Numbering dialog box, and select just one symbol. Enter the list, click after each item and select the desired symbol size..

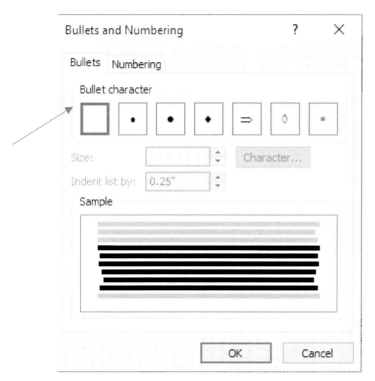

Figure: Choosing the Preferred Bullet Format

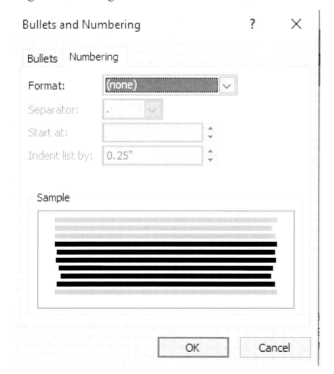

Figure: Choosing the preferred numbered list

Creating Numbered Lists

Numbered lists are used to distinguish each list item from the surrounding text and to make the list easier to read and recognize. Numbered lists are used when there is a hierarchy or priority between items. By default, Arabic numerals (1, 2, 3) are used, but other lists or numbering systems are possible, such as Roman numerals I ii, iii) and alphabetical lists (a, b, c).

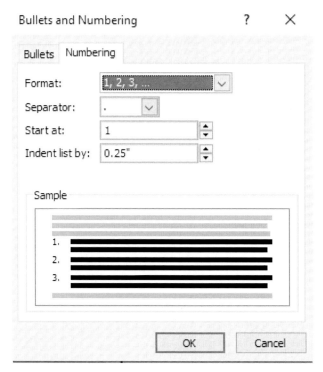

Figure: Choosing the preferred numbered list (1,2,3,..)

Click on page 4 in the page navigation area to view the last page of the publication.

Press 1 to start the numbered list. 2. 3. In the Paragraph category under Numbering in the main menu.

Type "escargot" and press

Enter each item in the list as shown, then click the button except for the last one. To make the text easier to read, click outside the text box.

To start a list with a number:

1. Click to start a new line.

• To adjust the spacing between each item in the list, use the Line Spacing option under Line Spacing in the Paragraph dialog box.

2. From the Paragraph category in the main menu, choose Numbering.

3. After selecting the numbering style you want, start typing the list and click after each item.

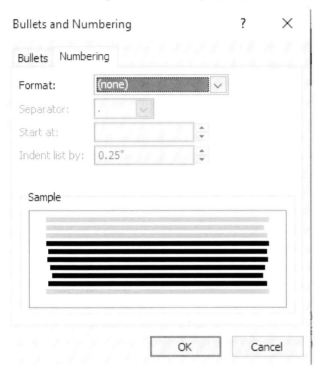

Creating Text Styles

Any text in your publication can be formatted with styles. A collection of styles organized under one name. Any text with this style applied will reflect the style changes. Styles can save you time and keep your magazines looking consistent.

- To open the New Style dialog box, on the Home tab, in the Styles group, click the Styles button, and then choose New Style. Enter the newsletter text here. Enter a new style name

- Times New Roman can be found by scrolling down and clicking the Fonts button to open the Fonts dialog box.

- Click [OK] to return to the New Style dialog box. Click the [Paragraph] button to display the Paragraph dialog box. Under General, click the Sort drop-down menu and select a sort. Basic instructions should now have a checkmark next to Text Alignment. Click OK. Click OK again to save the style and return to publishing..

Making a text style

1. On the Home tab, click the Styles button and choose a new style from the Styles group.

2. Choose the correct format.

3. Choose OK.

• Structured text for publication can serve as the basis for a style. To do this, select the formatted text, go to the New Style dialog box, name the style, make any necessary adjustments and click OK.

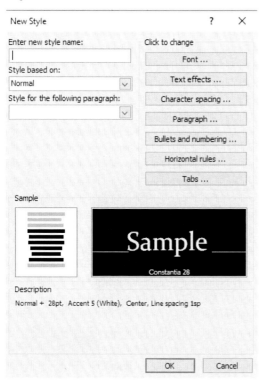

Applying A Text Style

- You can apply a style to text in a text box by first selecting the text and then choosing the desired style from the Style menu. When styles are applied to text, the formatting options affect how the content is displayed. Any formatting changes you make after applying the style will overwrite the formatting.

- Open Text Techniques 13.pub or the last file you used to continue this exercise. Select the full welcome article on the front page of your publication. To view a gallery of available styles, select a style from the Styles category on the Home tab. Scroll down and select the newsletter body for this article.

- To format the article, select the entire content of the slide and choose a body style for the newsletter. This format is used for the rest of the article on the next page.

- Drag the mouse away from the text box to clearly see the changes.

Using a text style

1. Select text.

2. Select a style by clicking the Style Groups link in the main menu.

- Styles can save you a lot of time if you regularly publish posts with the same text formatting options. For example, you can create text styles for titles, subheadings, body text, and notes, then apply them to the corresponding text boxes in each post.

Custom Font Schemes in Publisher: Overview

Publisher allows you to create custom font sets for use in your publications. You can create your own font schemes in Publisher by selecting the Page Design tab on the Ribbon. Then select "Font" from the drop-down menu in the "Table" button group. Select "Create New Font Scheme..." from the drop-down menu that appears and the "Create New Font Scheme" dialog box appears. To choose your own title and capitals for your own font scheme, click the drop-down button next to the Title Font: and Body Font: drop-down lists in the Create Font Scheme dialog box. You can name your own font scheme in the "Font scheme name:" text field. Then click "Save" to save the font suite.

Instructions for using Publisher custom font schemes: Screenshot of the Publisher Create New Font Scheme dialog box.

To use a custom font scheme in Publisher, select Page Design on the ribbon. Then select the Font button from the Table Buttons group. Then choose your own font scheme to use from the options that appear.

To delete a custom font scheme, click the Fonts button in the Editor's Table Buttons group. Custom font schemes can be removed from the right-click drop-down menu. Then choose "Delete Table" from the pop-up menu that opens. Select "Yes" in the confirmation dialog that appears to delete the custom font set.

Custom Font Schemes in Publisher: Instructions

1. To create a custom font scheme in Publisher, select Page Design on the ribbon.
2. Then select "Font" from the drop-down menu in the "Table" button group.
3. Select "Create New Font Scheme..." from the drop-down menu that appears to open the "Create New Font Scheme" dialog box.
4. To select your own title and uppercase fonts for the font scheme, click the drop-down buttons next to the Header Font: and Body Font: drop-down lists in the Create New Font Scheme dialog box.
5. Next, enter a unique font scheme name in the text box labeled "Font Scheme Name:".
6. Then click Save to save your custom font selection.
7. To use a custom font scheme in Publisher, select Page Design on the ribbon.
8. Then select the Font button from the group of buttons called Table.
9. From the displayed options, select your own font scheme to use.
10. To delete a custom font scheme from Publisher, select the Fonts button in the Scheme Buttons group.
11. Remove the custom font scheme by selecting Remove from the drop-down list that appears.
12. Then choose the "Delete Table" command from the pop-up menu that appears.
13. Select "Yes" in the confirmation dialog that appears to delete the custom font scheme.

Modifying A Text Style

After you create a style and apply it to multiple text boxes in your publication, you can decide if adjustments are needed. Fortunately, you can easily change an existing design instead of starting from scratch. When you do this, all text with the original style applied will immediately see the change.

• On the home page of your publication, select the text area for the welcome paragraph. To access the options menu, right-click the default newsletter style by clicking the Home tab, selecting Styles in the Styles group, and then selecting Styles.

Choose Modify to display the Modify Style dialog box. Press the up arrow on the first row indentation until "0.5 cm" appears. Click OK once, then OK again to make the necessary changes to your publication. The Paragraph dialog box opens.

All content currently using the default newsletter format will be updated to reflect the new writing style. Change of style:

1. Select the text box and apply the desired style.

2. On the Home tab, on the Styles page, in the Styles section, right-click the style you want to modify and select Modify.

3. Adjust the style components as needed.

• You can use templates to change styles. Right-click the style you want to modify, choose Update from the context menu, choose Customize Selection, and then choose a style from the Styles group on the Home tab.

Understanding the Layout Guides dialog box in Publisher

Layout standards are followed to facilitate coordination of journal components. The Layout Guides dialog box offers several suggestions, such as border guides, grid guides (such as column and row guides), reference guides, and ruler guides. The instructions are not printed, but are intended to help you organize your resources.

Layout Guides dialog

In the Layout Guides window, you may adjust the margin, grid, and baseline guides.

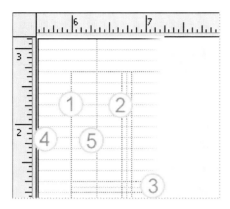

1.   guiding margins

2.   guide columns

3.   column guidelines

4.   Standard rules

5.   ruler directions

In Page Design > Guidelines, select Grids & Baselines to display the Layout Guide dialog box.

Use the Guides check box on the View tab to display the grid and margin guides. To display the baseline, check the Baseline box on the View tab.

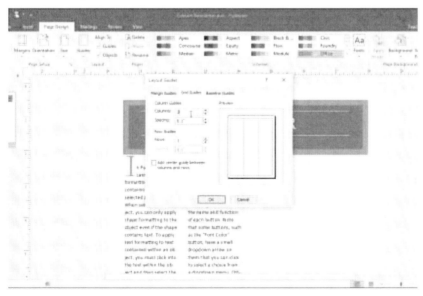

Press tab for margin guides

The margin guidelines allow you to manage how much space there is between a master page's boundaries. Each page to which it is applied displays the margin rules from the master page. Margin guides appear when the Boundaries and Guidelines option is active but the Ignore Master option is selected for a particular page.

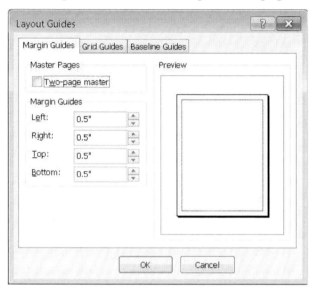

Master Pages

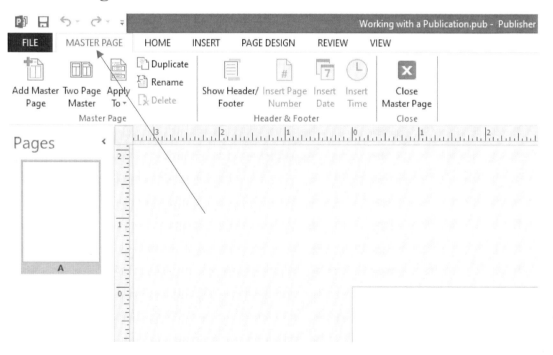

Master page two: Select this option to specify margins for a two-page spread if your publication is a book or pamphlet bound on one side. If you select this option, the left and right margin guidelines will change to the inner and outer margin guides. The book's bound edge is where you'll find the inner margin, and the fly edge is where you'll find the outside margin.

Guides for Margin

When you select a two-page layout, the Left and Right options change to Inside and Outside.

Left: Enter the desired distance between the left edge of the page and the left edge guide. The Double Page Templates check box lets you see how much space is left between the inside corners of the page and the guides inside the borders.

Right: Specifies the distance of the right edge guide from the edge of the page. You can check the Two Page Master check box to see how much space is left between the outer edge of the page and the outer edge guides.

Top: Specify the desired distance between the top margin guide and the margin at the top of

the page. Bottom: Specifies the space between the bottom margin guide and the edge of the page.

Remember that the unit of measurement you choose for your publication is the default, with margins set. Other units of measurement, such as inches (in), centimeters (cm), pi, points (pt), or pixels, can be specified by adding an integer value (px) followed by the appropriate abbreviation.

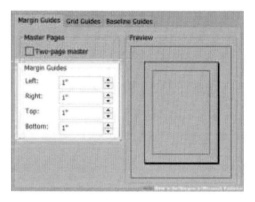

Tab for Grid Guides

Use the grid guidelines to set the number of columns and rows you want on your home page. Moderator Tip: The default distance value is displayed in the unit of measurement selected for the publication. You can specify other units of measurement by placing the appropriate abbreviation after the numeric value, such as inches (in), centimeters (cm), pi, points (pt), or pixels (px).

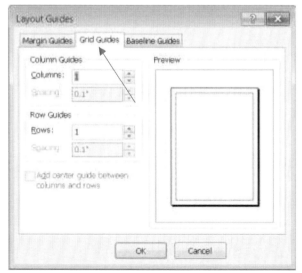

Layout Guide showing Column Guides

Column Guides

• You should provide the number of columns between the left and right margin specifications.

• Spacing Enter the desired distance between each column.

Guidelines for rows

• It is necessary to input the number of rows between the top and bottom margin guidelines.

• Spacing Enter the desired distance between each row.

• Add a center guide between the columns and rows. You have this option if there are several columns or rows. By selecting this option, you could see a nonprinting guide that indicates the ideal spacing between your columns and rows. Use this reference to position text boxes or graphical objects.

Baseline Guides tab

To match your text's baselines throughout each column in a multicolumn publication, use baseline guidelines.

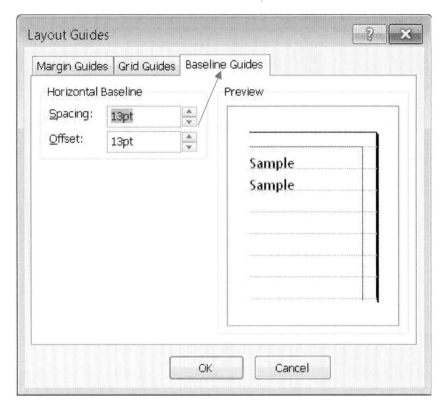

Figure: Baseline Guides

Horizontal baseline

Sets the offset and distance of the horizontal baseline.

The basic instructions are usually step-by-step and step-by-step. Even if you specify an alternate unit of measurement, such as inches, Publisher converts the value to a decimal.

In the Distance field, enter the appropriate distance between the horizontal baselines. The amount of line spacing in a paragraph you set to meet the minimum requirements is determined by how much you type.

Offset: Specifies the distance between the top edge guide and the next first horizontal base guide. The offset selection is affected by both the key spacing value in the main guide and the font size of the text. To bring the first line closer to the top of the page, you can make the offset value smaller than the spacing value if the font size is much smaller than the default spacing.

Chapter 6

Building Blocks!

In This Chapter

- All About Publisher Building Blocks
- Inserting Page Parts
- Inserting Calendars
- Inserting Borders and Accents
- Inserting Advertisements
- All About Pages and Adverts
- Understanding the Publisher Layout Building Blocks

INFOCUS

Building blocks are items that you may include into your publication, like as borders, headers, and sidebars. There are five types of building blocks: company information, calendars, borders and accents, advertising, and page components. These are all located in the Building Blocks category on the Insert tab. You may select from the pre-made construction blocks or make your own using a collection of items. Building blocks allow you to rapidly and with little effort produce an excellent magazine.

In this session you will:

- learn how to insert page parts
- learn how to insert a calendar
- learn how to insert borders and accents
- learn how to insert advertisements.

Inserting Page Parts

A page part is a class of structural elements that include headings, quotes, response forms, sidebars, stories, and content. These building blocks are useful when creating a publication from scratch because you can insert building blocks before adding content and modify them as needed. Try it yourself:

Open the file.

- This activity must start with a new, empty post. To view the options gallery
- Select the Insert tab, then select Page Part from the Building Blocks group.
- To display all topics, select All Topics. Then scroll down and select "Children". after,
- Click [Insert] to add this item to the document. To display the gallery of page elements
- Select Additional Page Components in the Building Blocks Library dialog box. Drag the title to the top of the page,
- Then scale to fit the page margins.
- Types of after-school programs and the Alpheius Global Enterprises Cultural Center
- As mentioned in the title. Remove placeholders for volume and newsletter data.
- Click anywhere outside the text to see the title clearly.

For your knowledge. To add page parts:

1. On the Insert tab, in the Components section, select Page Part.

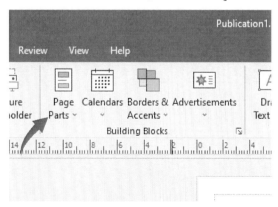

2. Click [Insert] after selecting More Page Pieces and after selecting one of the page parts.

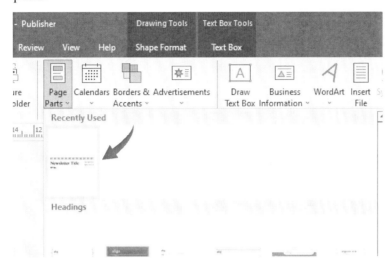

You may access the dialog box for the Building Block Library by choosing the Insert tab, followed by the dialog box launcher for the Building Blocks group.

Inserting Calendars

Publisher gives you the option to insert a calendar section instead of basing your entire publication on a calendar template. N.B. can be accessed. You can use these blocks to add dates, events, and events to any date in your calendar and add them to your document.

same file

Click the Insert tab, select Schedule from the Building Blocks group, and click More.

Calendar which opens the Calendar Gallery in the Building Blocks Library dialog box. Scroll to Studio, then click the drop-down arrow and click Studio. Select September from the list of months in the right panel and change the year to 2022..

• Click on **[Insert]** to insert the calendar into the publication

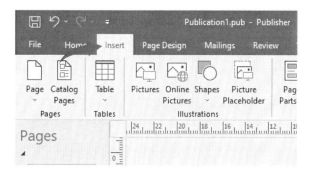

•   Click the **Calendars** icon in the Building Blocks group and click after the 1 in the box for Monday May 1st, press, then type Art

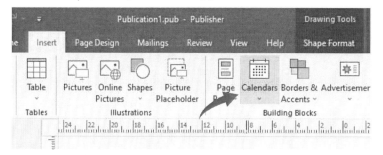

•   Repeat step 4 to type in each of the activities, as shown

•   Drag the calendar to the bottom of the page, then resize it to fit within the page margins

For Your Reference.

To insert a calendar:

1. Click on the Insert tab, then click on Calendars in the Building Blocks group

2. Click on a calendar, or Select More Calendars, click on a calendar, then click on [Insert]

• Instead of utilizing the Building Block Library dialog box, you may just click on Calendars in the Building Blocks group, then choose a calendar from the gallery to insert for the current or upcoming month.

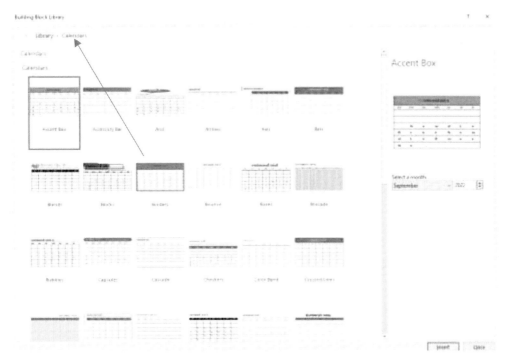

Figure: Creating a calendar

Inserting Borders And Accents

The Borders & Accents area includes a variety of architectural elements, including frames, bars, linear borders, emphasis borders, patterns, and boxes. These are designed to improve the appearance of your publication without taking away from the posted content.

To see the Borders & Accents gallery in the dialog box for the Building Block Library,

- Click the **Insert tab**

- Choose **Borders & Accents** from the Building Blocks group

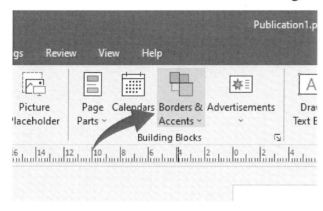

- Click More Borders and Accents.

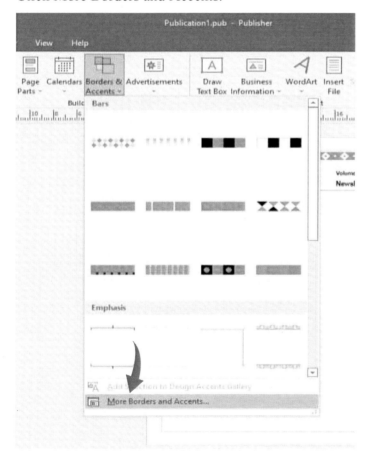

- Click on Banded Color in Frames 4 after scrolling to it.

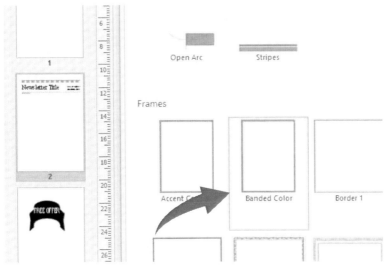

- To insert the border, click [Insert].

- To resize the border such that it sits just outside the page margins, click and drag the border's resize handles as demonstrated. To view the border in greater detail for your reference, click anywhere else in the magazine.

To add accents and borders:

1. Click Borders & Accents from the Insert menu's Building Blocks group. By clicking it, you may choose the accent or border you like. After selecting More Borders and Accents, click [Insert], then click the selected object.

2. If you frequently use the same borders and/or accents, you may quickly insert them by selecting the border or accent under Recently Used on the Insert tab and selecting Borders & Accents in the Building Blocks group.

Inserting Advertisements

Publisher separates the components for advertisements into three categories: ads, attention-

177

getters, and coupons. Ads that are intended to swiftly catch viewers' attention, such those that promote sales or amazing deals, fall under the heading of "Attention Getters."

the identical file

To make the Building Blocks Library dialog box's Ads gallery visible:

- Click the **Insert tab**

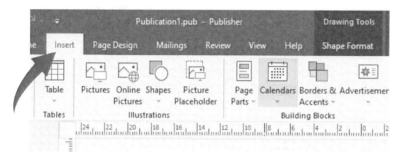

- Choose **Advertisements** from the Building Blocks group

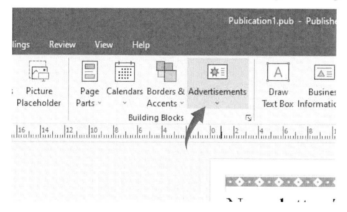

- Click More Advertisements. Select Hollowed Starburst from Attention Getters 24 by scrolling down.

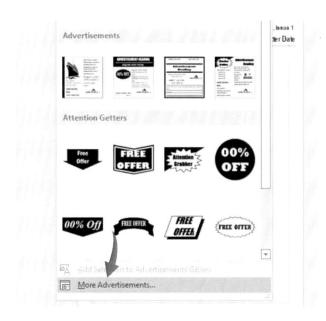

• To place the advertising, click [Insert].

• As demonstrated, resize the advertising, choose the wording, and then enter New Activities!

Click aside from the article to get a better view of the entire page.

For Your Information

To include a commercial:

1. From the Insert menu, choose Advertisements from the Building Blocks group.

2. After selecting the pertinent advertisement from the options list or from Select More Ads, click [Insert].

• A building block is inserted, and it fits the current color scheme of the publication. All elements of the publication will use the new colors if the publication's color scheme is altered.

179

Chapter 7

Working with Shapes!

In This Chapter

- All About Publisher Shapes
- Drawing and Inserting Shapes
- Selecting and Resizing Shapes
- Moving and Aligning Shapes
- Grouping Shapes and Changing Fill
- All About Drawing Lines
- Modifying and Deleting Publisher Shapes

INFOCUS

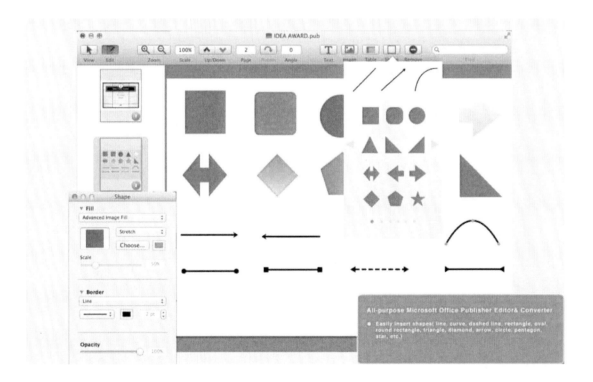

Using Publisher, you may create and include a range of pre-made forms into your publications.

While certain shapes complement other components, such as text boxes, nicely, others are more potent when used alone. Shapes are a very useful tool in Publisher since they can almost always be adjusted.

In this session, you will learn how to select, resize, move, align, and group shapes in addition to how to create and insert them. Additionally, you will discover how to add, delete, and edit lines in shapes.

Drawing And Inserting Shapes

It's easy to draw shapes and insert them. To insert a shape at the default size, just select the form from the Shapes collection and click once on the page. Choose the chosen form from the gallery, click where you want it on the page, and drag it there.

Use this as a test:

File Access

Working With Shapes 1.pub MUST be opened before starting this activity. the Shapes gallery may be seen:

- Click the **Insert tab**

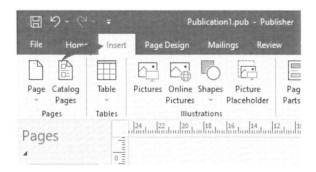

- Then select Shapes from the Illustrations group.

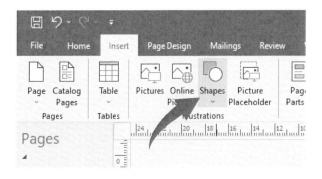

- In the Basic Shapes section (second row, second column), select the Cylinder form. To insert a cylinder at the default size, click once in the publication as shown.

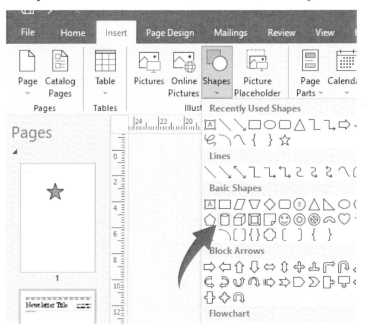

- To design two additional cylinders at a custom size, repeat steps 2 and 3 while selecting the Cylinder form. Do not worry about size at this time. Press to + undo after making a mistake when sketching, then try again.

For Your Information

Inserting a shape:

1. Select **Shapes** from the Illustrations category under the **Insert tab.**

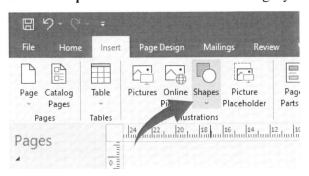

2. Select a shape.

3. Click to draw a shape of the default size, or Draw a custom-sized shape by dragging.

The Insert Shapes group in the Drawing Tools: Format tab's Shapes gallery is where you may access and insert shapes.

183

When you insert a shape, the Drawing Tools: Format tab becomes visible.

Selecting Shapes

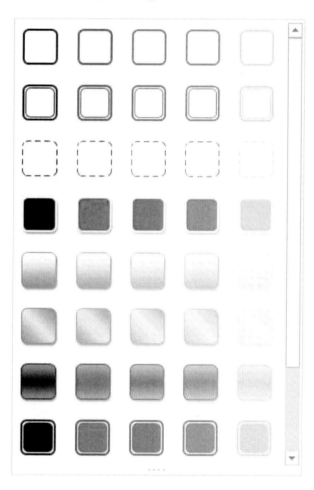

Before you can change a shape's properties, including moving, resizing, or formatting it, you must first pick the shape. When a shape is selected, a bounding box and control handles appear around it. The side and corner handles may be used for resizing, the top circular handle can be used for rotating, and the yellow handle can be used for editing.

Put This to the Test:

Equal File

To continue this exercise using the previous file, open the Working With Shapes 2.pub file. Click the first shape as shown. The form will have handles and a bounding box around it. Look for the three distinct handles, which are the white squares on the sides, the white circles on the corners, and the yellow diamond on curve 1. Just pick the biggest shape. The initial form won't be picked.

- Once the first shape has been chosen, hold down CTRL and click the other two shapes. All three of the forms will be chosen, and if necessary, formatted, simultaneously.
- Click anywhere on the page to deselect the shapes.

For Your Information

Unchecking a shape:

If you have numerous shapes chosen, you may deselect one shape at a time by holding down the mouse button while clicking on the shape you wish to deselect. • Click outside the shape.

Resizing Shapes

There may be times when you need to adjust the size of a shape you've drawn. There are several ways to do this. One option is to use the control handles to resize a shape manually. Alternatively, you can use the Size controls in the Size group on the Drawing Tools: Format tab to incrementally increase or decrease the width and/or height of the shape.

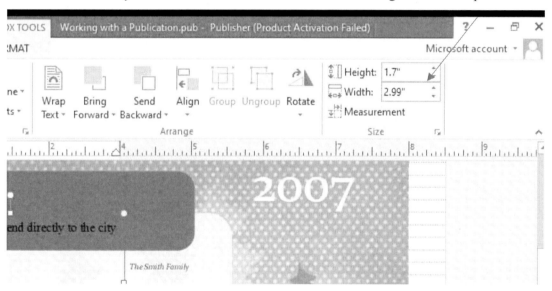

Figure: Resizing shapes' dimensions (height and width)

Try This Yourself:

Same File

• Select the tall, thin shape, then point to the top left corner of the shape until a two-headed arrow pointer appears, as shown

• Click and drag down to resize the shape

• Select the large shape and drag the side handles inwards until it appears. Let's resize these shapes accurately

• Select the left shape, click on the Drawing Tools:

• Format tab, then click on the up spinner arrow for Height in the Size group until it reaches 3.8 cm

• Take note of the Width of the shape

• Select the right shape, then repeat step 4 to apply the same Height and Width as the left shape

• Click anywhere on the page to deselect the shape

For Your Reference

To resize a shape:

1. Select a shape

2. Drag the control handles, or Click on the Drawing Tools: Format tab, then adjust the values in Height or Width in the Size group

• If you wanted to create shapes that were all the same size you could select all of the shapes, click on the Drawing Tools: Format tab, then click in the Height and Width boxes in the Size group and type the desired values.

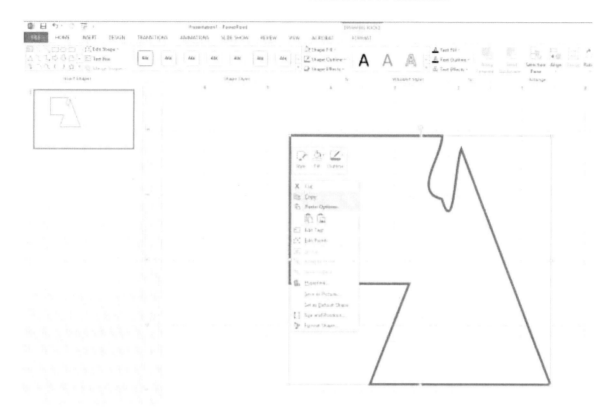

Moving Shapes

You'll probably need to make minor modifications to the location of the form when you create it on the page or in the drawing canvas. By dragging it with the mouse or the arrow keys in Publisher, you may move a shape across a page.

Put This to the Test:

Same File

Open the file or use the previous one to continue with this task. Understanding Shapes 4.pub.

Choose the left shape.

Select the left shape.

•   Press the arrow keys ( ) repeatedly until the shape is positioned approximately as shown

•   Click on the right shape to select it, then press the arrow keys repeatedly until the shape is positioned as shown

•   Shapes and drawings can also be moved by dragging with the mouse.

•   Select all three shapes and drag to the right

For Your Reference

To move a shape:

1. Click on the shape or drawing to select it

2. Drag it with the mouse, or Use the arrow keys to move it around

• If you move a shape by dragging it, pink guidelines will appear when the shape aligns with other objects on the page.

Aligning Shapes

When you use multiple shapes in a publication, you may need to ensure they are accurately aligned with each other. You can do this by using the Align tool on the Home and Drawing Tools: Format tabs, or by dragging the shapes until the pink guidelines appear.

Try This Yourself:

Same File

Continue using the previous file with this exercise, or open the file Working With Shapes_5.pub...

•   Ensure the two larger shapes are selected

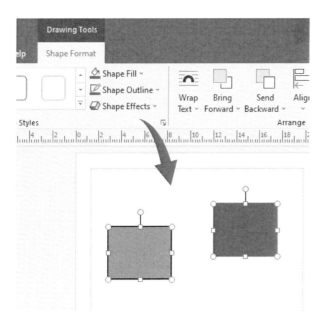

• Click on the Drawing Tools: Format tab, then click on **Align** in the **Arrange group** to display a menu of options

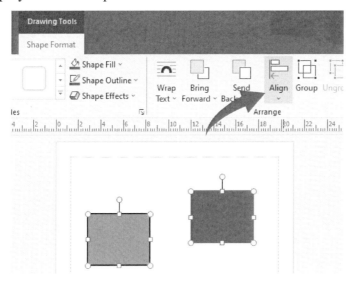

• Select **Align Bottom** to align the bottom of the shapes with each other, as shown.

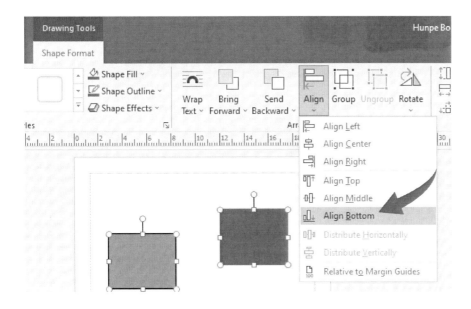

Let's use another method to align the other shape. Select the third shape

• Drag the shape up and to the left until a pink guideline appears along the bottom of all three shapes, as shown, then release the mouse button

• Click elsewhere in the publication to deselect the shapes

For Your Reference.

To align shapes:

• Select the shapes to be aligned, click on the Drawing Tools: Format tab, click on Align in the Arrange group, then select the desired alignment option; or

• Drag each shape until they are aligned along the pink guideline

• You can align shapes to the middle or edges of the page, rather than in relation to each other. To do this, click on the Drawing Tools: Format tab, click on Align in the Arrange group, then select Relative to Margin Guides.

Grouping Shapes

When working with multiple shapes, such as where you have drawn several individual shapes to make up a single diagram, you may find it easier to group the shapes. Grouped shapes act as a single object and, as such, can be moved, aligned and formatted as a single object.

Try This Yourself:

Same File

Continue using the previous file with this exercise, or open the file Working With Shapes_6.pub. Select all three shapes

• Click on the on the shape you will like to group as one as shown below and then, Drawing Tools: Format tab.

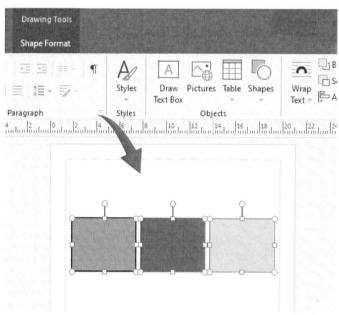

• Then click on **Group** in the **Arrange group**. The shapes will be contained within the one bounding box and treated as a single object.

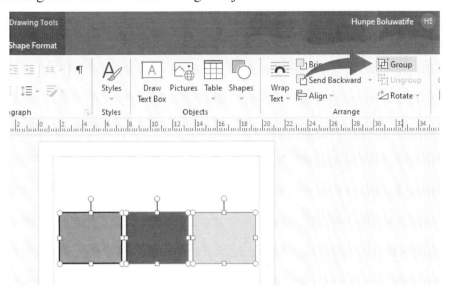

• Select the bounding box for the grouped shapes, then point to the **top right corner** until a two-headed arrow appears

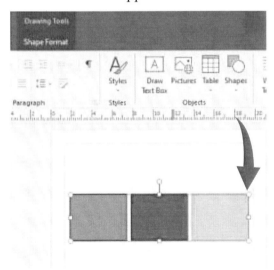

- Drag up diagonally to resize all three shapes, as shown. The shapes are resized as one object

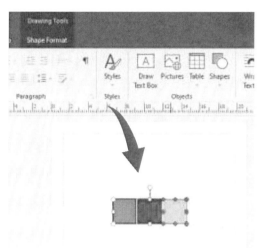

- On the Drawing Tools: Format tab, click on **Ungroup** in the Arrange group to ungroup the shapes

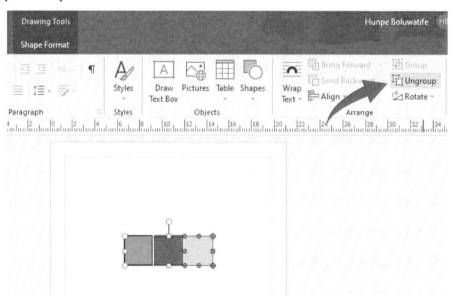

For Your Reference.

To group or ungroup shapes:

1. Select the shapes, then click on the Drawing Tools: Format tab

2. Click on Group in the Arrange group to group the shapes, or Click on Ungroup in the Arrange group to ungroup the shapes

To quickly group or ungroup shapes, right-click on the selected shapes to display a shortcut menu, select either Group or Ungroup.

Changing Fill

Shapes that you draw or put into a publication by default have a solid fill. Almost anything you desire may be used as this fill, including a gradient, texture, pattern, image, or nothing at all. The Fill Effects dialog box may be used to do all of this.

Put This to the Test

Same File

Open the file Working With Shapes 7.pub or carry on with the previous file for this practice. Pick the more compact form.

•   Select the shape you like to change the fill

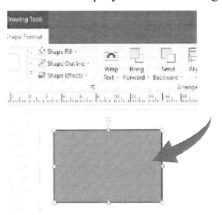

- Select Gradient fill by clicking on the Drawing Tools: Format tab,

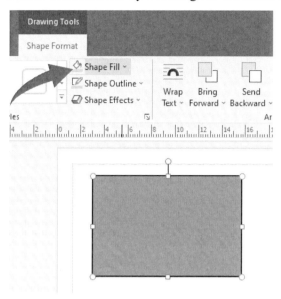

- then click the Shape Styles group's dialog box launcher to open the Format AutoShape dialog box.

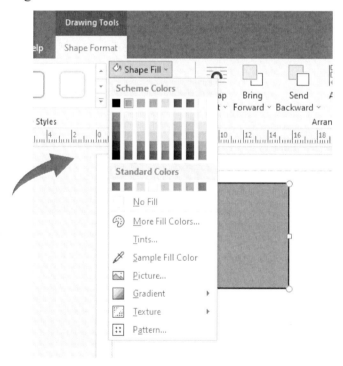

- Select Medium Gradient - Accent 1 by clicking on the drop-down arrow under Preset gradients.

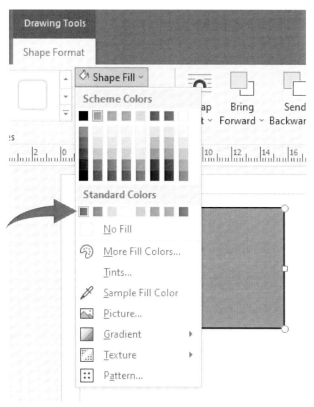

- Click on [OK], then click on [OK] again to apply the change

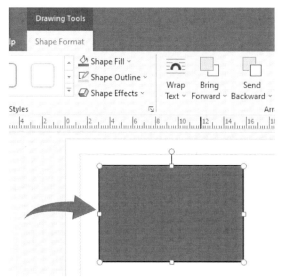

For Your Information

In order to modify a shape's fill:

1. Select the shape, select the Drawing Tools: Format tab, and then select the Shape Styles group's dialog box launcher.

2. After making the appropriate modifications, click [OK].

You may easily alter a shape's fill color by selecting the Drawing Tools: Format tab, Shape Fill in the Shape Styles group, and then a different color from the drop-down menu.

Drawing Lines

In publishing, lines can be used to separate pages into sections, as part of a design, or to give a page structure. Additionally, they can be utilized in forms to include a writing section. The Line tool, the Arrow tool, as well as the Double Arrow, Curve, Freeform, and Scribble tools that are found in the Shapes menu, are all available for creating lines in Publisher.

Put This to the Test:

Same File

Open the file Working With Shapes 8.pub if you want to continue with the previous file for this exercise.

- Click on the **Insert tab**

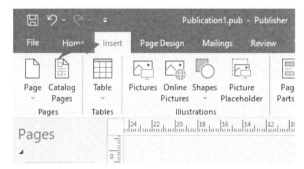

- Click on Shapes

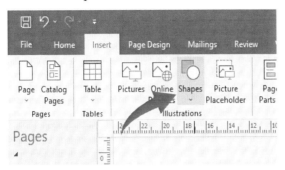

- Select Line from the Lines group under the Illustrations group in the Shapes section of the Insert tab. The cursor will turn into a cross.

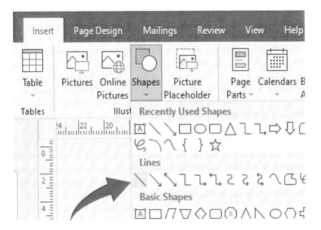

- To create a horizontal line across the page, hold down the mouse button while clicking and dragging.

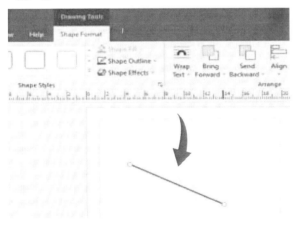

- Holding down makes sure that the line is drawn straight. Until the mouse button is released, the line will be dashed.

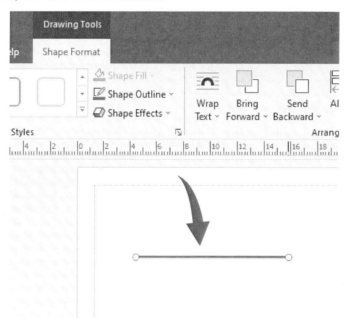

- To draw a vertical line on the right side of the page, repeat steps 1 and 2 as displayed.

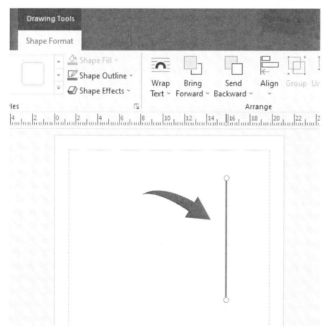

- Deselect the line by clicking anywhere else in the article to clearly see the changes.

For Your Information

Drawing lines

1.   Select Shapes from the Illustrations category under the Insert tab.

2.   Hold down if you need a straight line.

3.   Draw the line as necessary by clicking and dragging.

•   Compared to the other line tools, the Curve and Freeform tools operate significantly differently. Select the line's beginning point by clicking, then select the line's anchor point by clicking once more. Up until the line is finished, keep moving the mouse and clicking at the anchor points.

Deleting Shapes

You could occasionally determine that a form belongs in a new or old publication, but you need to delete it. Fortunately, removing a shape only requires selecting it and hitting the or key. If text wrapping is enabled for the form, the text will resize to take up any extra room.

Put This to the Test:

Same File

Open the file or use the previous one to continue with this task. Understanding Shapes 9.pub...

•   We want to delete the shape on the left hand side. The rectangle.

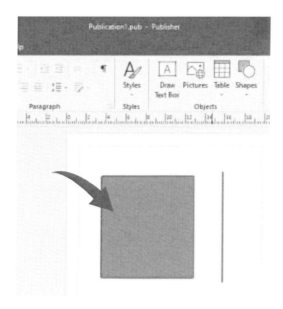

•   Click on the left-hand shape.

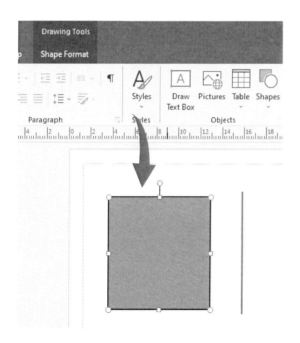

•   Press delete

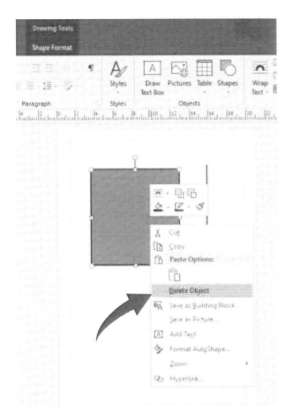

- The shape is removed from the publication;

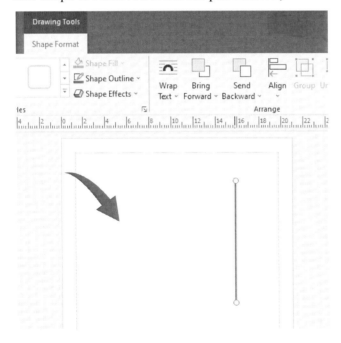

- To restore it, click Undo in the QAT;

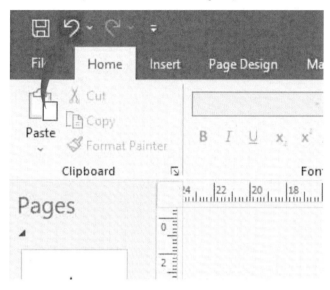

- To select all of the forms, press 2;

The two shapes have been eliminated from the text.

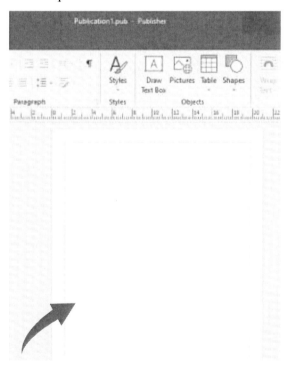

Chapter 8

Working with Pictures!

In This Chapter

- All About Publisher Pictures
- Inserting Pictures
- Inserting Online Pictures
- Using the Scratch Area
- Swapping Pictures
- Picture Formatting and Effects
- Cropping Pictures and Inserting Captions

INFOCUS

Pictures are an important part of working with Publisher. Most of the publications you create will probably need pictures in them – a flyer or a newsletter would most likely look rather boring with only text.

Pictures also enable you to communicate visually to your reader, which can sometimes say much more than text alone.

In this session you will:

- learn how to insert pictures
- learn how to insert online pictures
- learn how to use the scratch area
- learn how to swap pictures
- learn how to apply formatting and effects to pictures
- learn how to crop pictures
- learn how to insert captions.

Inserting Pictures

Knowing how to insert pictures is an important aspect of working with Publisher. Pictures help to draw attention to a publication and to illustrate your points. To insert a picture from your computer, the picture must be stored somewhere on your computer and must be in a relevant file format (such as .jpg or .bmp).

Try This Yourself:

Open File

Before starting this exercise you MUST open the file Working With Pictures_1.pub...

*   Ensure page 1 of the publication is displayed
*   Click on the Insert tab, then click on Pictures in the Illustrations group to display the Insert Picture dialog box
*   Navigate to the course files folder, then click on Cogs.bmp 3
*   Click on [Insert] to insert the picture into the publication 5
*   Drag the picture to the top of the page, as shown
*   Use the resize handles to resize the picture, as shown
*   Click elsewhere in the publication to deselect the picture

For Your Reference

To insert a picture:

1. Click on the Insert tab, then click on Pictures in the Illustrations group

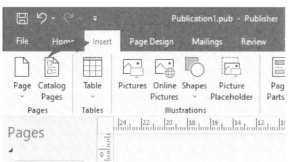

2. Select the Pictures icon as shown in the image below.

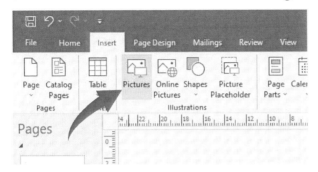

3. Navigate to the desired picture file, then click on [Insert]

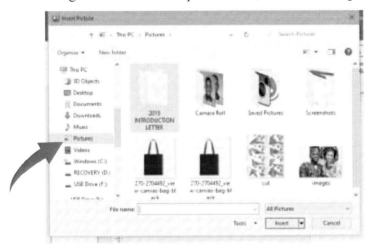

• You can accurately resize a picture by selecting it, then clicking on the Picture Tools: Format tab. You can specify the exact Height and Width in the Size group on this tab.

Inserting Online Pictures

Publisher allows you to enter images without first saving them to your computer, in addition to allowing you to insert images from your local computer and a number of web sources.

You may enter images online by using a Bing search, your own OneDrive, or Flickr account.

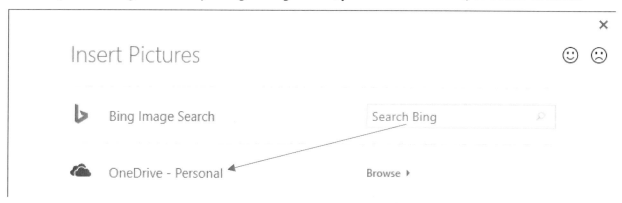

Figure: Using Online Pictures in Publisher

Try This Yourself:

Same File

Continue using the previous file with this exercise, or open the file Working With Pictures_2.pub...

- Click on the Insert tab

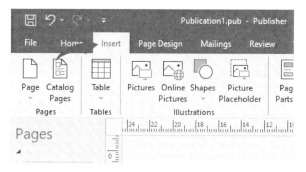

- Click on Online Pictures in the Illustrations group to display the Insert Pictures pane

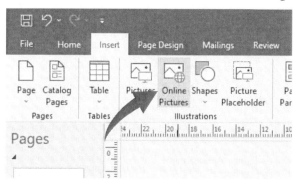

- Click in the Search Bing search box, then type **palette**

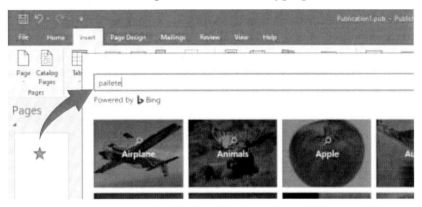

- The search will return thousands of ClipArt images pertaining to art…

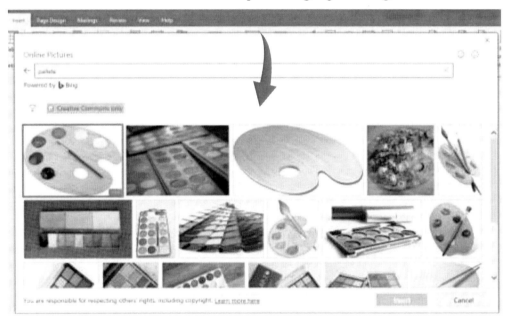

- Click on an image of an artist's palette, as shown

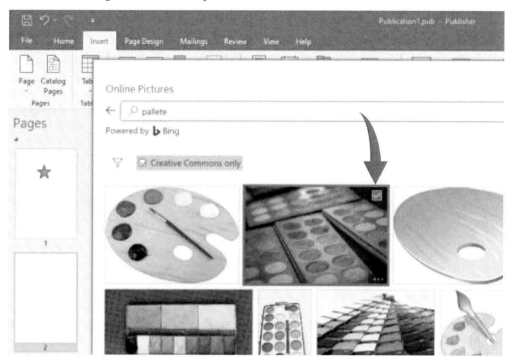

- Click on [Insert] to insert the picture into the publication

- Drag the picture across to the right pane of the brochure, then resize it, as shown

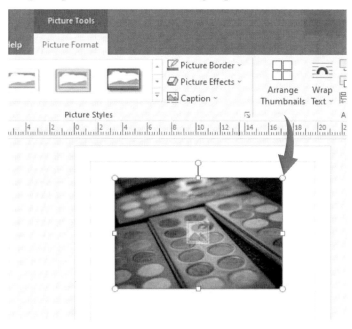

- Deselect the picture to see the publication more clearly

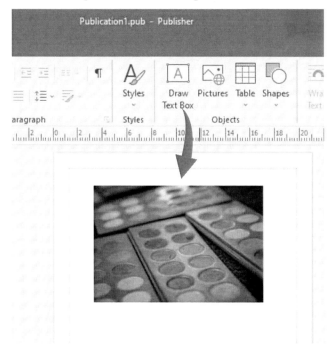

For Your Reference

To insert an online picture:

1. Click on the Insert tab, then click on Online Pictures in the Illustrations group

2. Locate and click on the desired picture, then click on [Insert]

Be careful when using online pictures in your publication. Some online pictures are copyrighted, and there may be restrictions on whether or not you can legally use them in a publication.

Using The Scratch Area

The grey border that surrounds the page in the publishing window is the scratch area. For things like photographs and text boxes, this section may be utilized as a type of storage space, making it simple to move items about and experiment with positions without continually adding and removing things.

When you switch pages, items stay in the scratch area.

Put This to the Test:

File Opening

You MUST open the file Working With Pictures 3.pub before beginning this activity.

Ensure the first page of the publication is displayed

Some images have been inserted into the middle panel of this page

•   Select the pencil picture by clicking on it, then drag it to the page's left-hand scratch area as demonstrated.

•   To view Page 2 of the publication, click on it in the Pages navigation bar. In the scratched region, the pencils' image is still visible.

•   In the right panel, underneath the phrase Seniors Classes, drag the image into the page.

•   To reveal the first page in the Pages navigation bar, click on it. To choose it, click on the handprints picture.

•   Drag the picture to the scratch area while holding down.

•   The image is copied to the scratch area

For Your Reference

To move a picture to the scratch area:

•   Drag the picture into the scratch area

To copy a picture to the scratch area:

•   Select the picture, hold down

•   If you insert more than one picture at a time into a publication, the pictures will initially appear in the scratch area rather than on the page, then drag the picture to the scratch area

•   You can turn the scratch area on and off by clicking on the View tab, then clicking on Scratch Area in the Show group.

Swapping Pictures

There may be times when you have inserted two pictures into a publication and then realized that they would look better if they swapped places. Fortunately, Publisher has a swap function that saves you from dragging and repositioning pictures. You can swap pictures within the pages of a publication, in the scratch area, or between the pages and the scratch area.

Try This Yourself:

Same File

Continue using the previous file with this exercise, or open the file Working With Pictures_4.pub...

- Click on the picture of the camera to select it, then point to the middle of the picture. Notice there is an icon in the middle of the picture, which looks like two mountains and an arrow

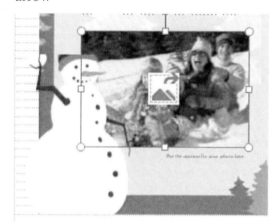

- Click on the icon and drag to the right to point to the handprint picture until it appears with a pink border, as shown

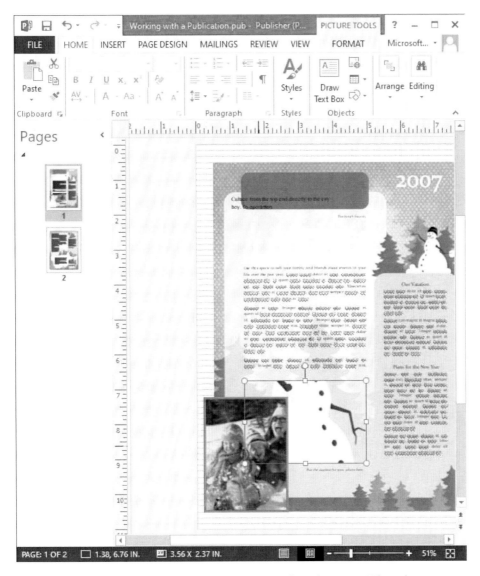

- Release the mouse button to swap the pictures. The pictures were slightly different sizes, so part of the camera image was cut off

- Repeat steps 1 to 3 to swap the picture of the camera with the picture in the scratch area

- Repeat steps 1 to 3 to swap the picture of the camera with the handprint picture on the left

The camera picture is returned to its original position

For Your Reference

To swap pictures:

1. Select a picture, then point to the swap icon in the middle of the picture

2. Click and drag to the picture to be swapped with until it appears with a pink border

3. Release the mouse button

• When swapping pictures, ensure that both pictures are of similar height and width. When the swap takes place, each picture will take on the format of the picture it was swapped with, which can cause parts of pictures to be cut off and other strange results.

Picture Formatting And Effects

Publisher provides you with a range of effects and formatting options for pictures to help you enhance the appearance of your publications. These effects include color correction, recoloring, borders, shadows, reflections and so on, and are available on the Picture Tools: Format tab.

Try This Yourself:

Same File

Continue using the previous file with this exercise, or open the file Working With Pictures_5.pub...

•　　　Select the picture of the cogs at the top of the page. This picture is a different shade of purple to the shades in the active color scheme

•　　　Click on the Picture Tools: Format tab, then click on Recolor in the Adjust group. A gallery of options relevant to the color scheme is displayed

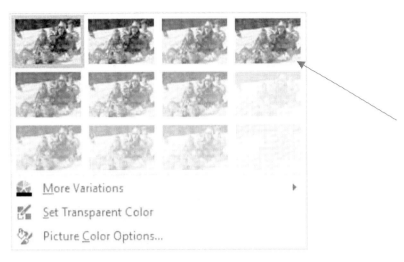

More Variations ▶

Set Transparent Color

Picture Color Options...

- Click on RGB (230, 204, 230), Accent color Dark in the third column of the second row to recolor the picture

- Select the picture of the paint palette, then on the Picture Tools: Format tab, click on Picture Effects in the Picture Styles group to display a menu of options

- Point to Soft Edges, then select 10 Point

- Click away from the picture to see the changes more clearly

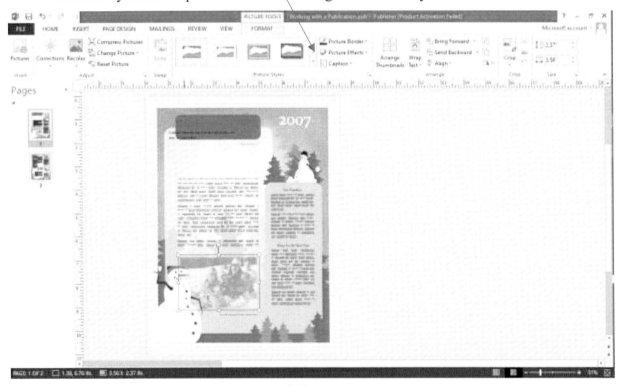

For Your Reference

To apply formatting or effects to pictures:

1. Select the picture

2. Click on the Picture Tools: Format tab

3. Navigate to the desired format or effect, then select it

• When applying effects to a picture, be careful not to go overboard. Too many effects can detract from the picture itself and lower the quality of your publication.

Cropping Pictures

There may be times when you insert a picture which takes up too much room, or when you only need part of an image. Publisher allows you to crop a picture, similar to cutting a photograph to fit it into a frame. Unlike cutting a photo, however, cropping is easily reversed if a mistake is made.

Try This Yourself:

Same File

Continue using the previous file with this exercise, or open the file Working With Pictures_6.pub...

•   Select the picture of the snowman on the first page of the publication

•   Click on the Picture Tools: Format tab, then click on the top half of Crop in the Crop group

•   Black crop handles appear around the picture.

•   Point to the crop handle in the middle of the top edge of the picture until the mouse pointer changes to a crop handle. Let's crop out the excess white space at the top of the picture.

•   Click and drag the top middle crop handle down, then release the mouse button to crop the picture, as shown

- On the Picture Tools: Format tab, click on the top half of Crop in the Crop group again to finish cropping

- Click and drag the picture up so that it doesn't overlap the border, as shown

- Click away from the picture to see the changes more clearly

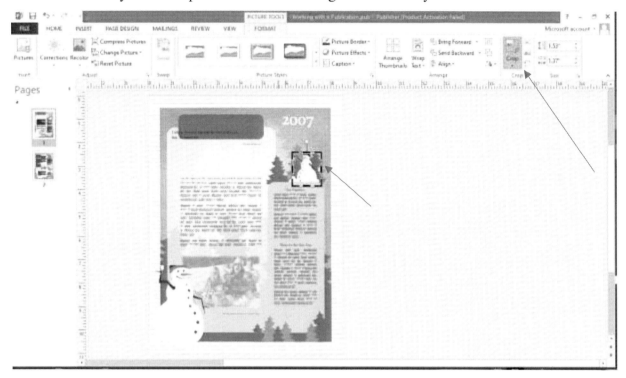

For Your Reference

To crop a picture:

1. Select the picture, click on the Picture Tools: Format tab, then click on the top half of Crop in the Crop group

2. Click and drag the crop handles to crop the picture as desired

3. Click on Crop again to finish cropping

• When you crop a picture, the parts you crop out won't completely disappear straight away; they will just be greyed out until you click on Crop or press to finish cropping. This allows you to modify the cropping if necessary.

Inserting A Caption

A caption is a small piece of text that describes or provides information about an image, diagram or something similar. It is very simple to add a caption to a picture in Publisher, and there are several design options to choose from, including colors, waves, and even captions written vertically rather than horizontally.

Try This Yourself:

Same File

Continue using the previous file with this exercise, or open the file Working With Pictures_7.pub...

- Select the picture of the Snowman on the first page of the publication
- Click on the Picture Tools: Format tab, then click on Caption in the Picture Styles group to display a gallery of options

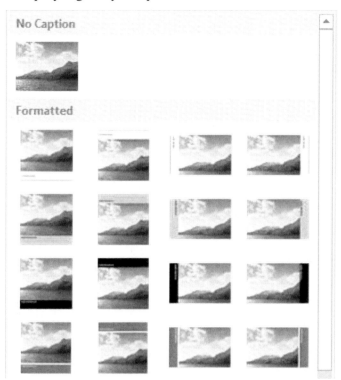

- Click on the first option under Formatted; A caption box will appear below the picture.

- Click in the caption box, then type Frank showing off their artwork

- Click away from the picture to see the caption more clearly

For Your Reference

To insert a caption:

1. Select the picture to be captioned

2. Click on the Picture Tools: Format tab, click on Caption in the Picture Styles group, then select an option

3. Click in the caption box, then type the caption

• Captions are usually quite short. Because of this, caption boxes are small and only hold one line of text. If you are inserting a caption and your text does not fit, consider rewording your text to make it smaller, or try inserting a small text box below the picture instead.

Chapter 9

Working with Tables!

In This Chapter

- All About Publisher Tables
- Inserting Tables
- Entering Text in a Table
- Adjusting Rows and Columns
- Applying Table Styles
- Using Fills and Tints
- Using Simple Fill Color

INFOCUS

Tables are grids of rows and columns that are typically used for organizing information such as order forms, price lists, and statistics.

Like text boxes and pictures, tables that you create in Publisher are objects, and are therefore easy to move, resize, and modify.

In this session you will:

- learn how to insert a table
- learn how to enter text in a table
- learn how to adjust rows and columns
- learn how to apply table styles
- learn how to apply fill and tints
- learn how to use Sample Fill Color.

Inserting Tables

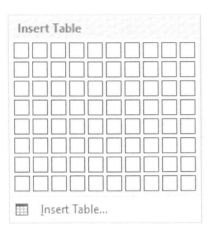

In Publisher, making a table is as easy as choosing the number of rows and columns. Although it is desirable to know the dimensions you need before creating the table, if required, you may easily add or remove rows afterwards. Tables may be changed in the same ways as images and text boxes since they are objects exactly like them.

Try This Yourself:

Open File

You MUST open the file Tables 1.pub before beginning this activity.

- To open the Create Table dialog box,

- click the Insert tab, choose the Tables group, and then click Table.

- Input 8 for the number of rows, press, and then type 4 for the number of columns, as indicated.

- Click [OK] to insert the table, then click and drag it to the desired location by pointing at the table's edge until a four-headed arrow appears on the mouse pointer.

- Click away from the table to deselect it.

- Point to the center of the bottom edge of the table until the mouse cursor turns into a double headed arrow, and then click and drag to enlarge the table.

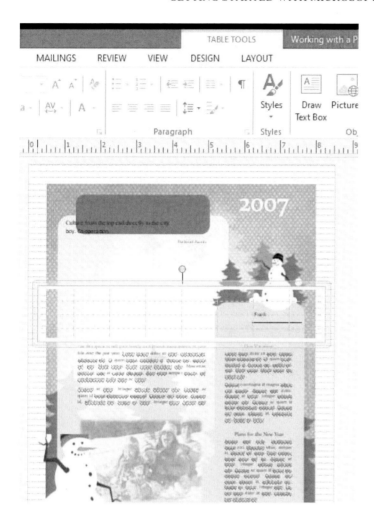

For Your Reference

To insert a table:

1. Click on the Insert tab, click on Table in the Tables group, then select Insert Table

2. Specify the number of rows and columns required, then click on [OK]

• If you click on the Insert tab, then click on Table in the Tables group, a grid is displayed in the menu. You can quickly insert a table by selecting the number of rows and columns in the grid.

Entering Text In A Table

A table's cells resemble separate text boxes. Simply click within a cell and begin typing to enter content there. The insertion point will shift to the following cell when you press be formatted similarly to text in text boxes—you may modify the font, size, style, color, and other formatting options.

Try This Yourself:

Same File

Continue using the previous file with this exercise, or open the file Tables_2.pub...

- To place the insertion point, click in the first cell at the top left of the table.

- Press after typing Production to change the insertion point to the following cell.

- Repetition of step 2 is necessary to enter the heads into the second, third, and fourth cells. The insertion point shifts to the first cell of the following row when you push at the end of a row.

- Click on the Home tab, click on the drop arrow for Font Size in the Font group, then pick 16 to raise the text size.

- Click on the top left cell, then click and drag to the bottom right cell to select every cell in the table. Fill up the table as indicated.

- Repeat step 4 to select the top row of the table, then, on the Home tab, click on Bold in the Font group

- Click away from the table to see the text more clearly

For Your Reference

To enter text into a table:

1. Click in the cell that will hold the text

2. Type the text

3. Press enter

• You can pre-format table cells so that any text inserted in them will automatically have the required font, size, style, and alignment.

Adjusting Rows And Columns

Rows and/or columns may need to be added, removed, or adjusted in order to match the available space and the text they contain. To avoid changing the data in the table too much, Publisher lets you add rows and columns at any place in the table, and changing the size of rows and columns is as easy as clicking and dragging.

Try This Yourself:

Same File

Continue using the previous file with this exercise, or open the file Tables_3.pub...

- Click in the cell containing the text Lorene Devoir in Concert. This is the first cell in the bottom row. Let's insert a new row below this one

- Click on the Table Tools: Layout tab, then click on Insert Below in the Rows & Columns group to insert a new row. The new row causes the table to extend past the bottom page margin.

- Point to the gridline between the first and second rows so the mouse pointer changes to a double- headed arrow, then click and drag the gridline up to resize the first row

- Ensure the bottom row of the table is selected, then on the Table Tools: Layout tab, click on Merge Cells in the Merge group. The four cells merge to become one cell.

- Type *Proof of Concession required, then click away from the table to see the changes more clearly

For Your Reference

To insert a row or a column:

1. Click in a cell adjacent to where the new row or column is to be inserted

2. Click on the Table Tools: Layout tab, then click on the appropriate option in the Rows &

Columns group

To adjust a row or column:

1. Click on the gridline between two rows or columns

2. Drag the gridline up, down, left or right as required.

Applying Table Styles

Publisher provides you with an assortment of table style options designed to enhance the appearance of your table. These include different display options for gridlines, as well as options for coloring rows and columns. The range of colors that are available is determined by the active color scheme.

Try This Yourself:

Same File

Continue using the previous file with this exercise, or open the file Tables_4.pub.

- Ensure the table is selected, then click on the Table Tools: Design tab

- In the Table Formats group, click on the More arrow for the Table Styles gallery to see the range of available table styles

- Select Table Style 22 to apply this style to the table 24

- Click away from the table to see the changes more clearly

For Your Reference

To apply a table style:

1. Select the table, then click on the Table Tools: Design tab

2. Click on the More arrow for the Table Styles gallery in the Table Formats group

3. Select a style from the gallery

• Different table styles will be appropriate for different kinds of tables; for example, a class timetable might have the left column colored the same way as the top row, while a business form probably would not.

Using Fills And Tints

In addition to utilizing the pre-defined styles, you may pick your own fill colors for the table's rows, columns, or individual cells before selecting various nuances or shades of those colors. The current color scheme and the type of information being housed in the table will determine the colors and color variants you employ.

Try This Yourself:

Same File

Continue using the previous file with this exercise, or open the file Tables_5.pub.

- Pick the table's third row. This argument centers on the pricing of tickets for the Great Mozart.
- To view a gallery of possibilities, select the Table Tools: Design tab, then select the Fill in the Table Formats group's bottom half.
- Accent 2 (RGB (204, 204, 0)) should be selected.
- Click on a separate cell to view the color more fully, then lighter 40% to apply this fill color to the row.
- Select the row once more since it's a touch too bright.

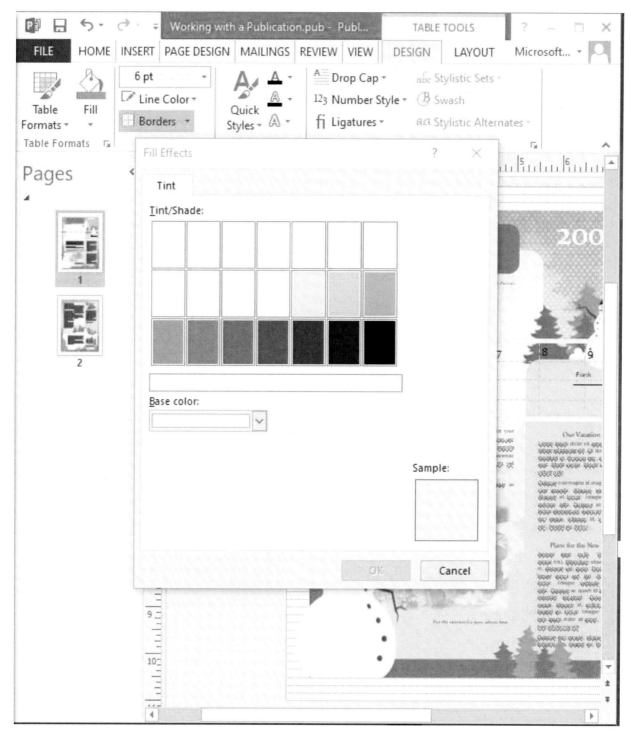

Repeat step 2, then select Tints to display the Fill Effects dialog box 7

We can now choose a different tint of the same color to fill the row.

- Click on 30% Tint (the fourth option in the top row), then click on [OK]
- Click away from the table to see the changes

For Your Reference

To apply a fill color to a table:

1. Choose the cells you want to color
2. Select the Table Tools: Design tab, then select the Fill in the Table Formats group's bottom half.
3. Decide on the preferred color.

- To create a tint, combine a color with white. One portion of the original hue and nine parts of white make up a 10% tint.
- Shades are colors blended with black. One component of the original hue and nine parts of black make up a 10% shade.

Using Sample Fill Color

You could occasionally find a fill color you like but be unclear of where to look to utilize it again. As an alternative, you could have altered a fill color and wish to utilize it again without spending time making all of the changes over. In these situations, the Sample Fill Color tool is a helpful feature that enables you to quickly and efficiently reuse a color.

Try This Yourself:

Same File

Continue using the previous file with this exercise, or open the file Tables_6.pub.

- Select the fifth row of the table, with the ticket prices for Spartacus
- Click on the Table Tools: Design tab, click on the bottom half of Fill in the Table Formats group, then select Sample Fill Color

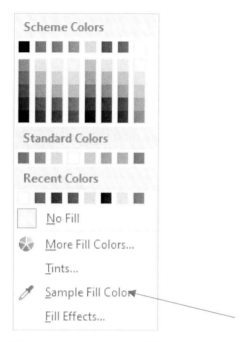

The mouse pointer will change to a small dropper icon.

•   Click in the cell containing the text Magnificent Mozart to apply the fill color from this cell to the selected cells

•   Click in another cell to see the color more clearly

•   Repeat steps 1 to 4 to apply the fill color to the row containing the ticket prices for Giselle

For Your Reference

To use Sample Fill Color:

1.   Select the cells to apply the fill color to

2.   Click on the Table Tools: Design tab, click on the bottom half of Fill in the Table Formats group, then select Sample Fill Color

3.   Click on the desired color on the page

• You can use the Sample Fill Color tool on almost any color on a page, including a cell fill, the page background, or even text.

• When you use the Sample Fill Color tool, the color you sample appears under Recent Colors, making it quick and easy to find it and use it again.

Chapter 10

Publisher Design and Layout!

∎∎∎

In This Chapter

- All About Design and Layout
- Understanding Page Sizes and Orientation
- Creating Envelopes and Labels
- Creating Folder Cards and Grid Guides
- Changing Margin Guides
- Creating and Using Ruler Guides
- Using Color and Font Schemes
- Creating a Fill and Image Background

∎∎∎

INFOCUS

There is much more to a publication than the visual elements such as the pictures and text. The "skeleton" of a publication, as it were, consists of the foundations that these elements are built onto, such as page size and orientation, margins and guides. These layout elements, along with design elements such as color schemes, font schemes and backgrounds, provide a basis for your publication to which you can then go on to add objects and information.

In this session you will:

- learn how to change the page orientation
- gain an understanding of page sizes
- learn how to create envelopes
- learn how to create folded cards
- learn how to change margin guides

- learn how to create grid guides

- learn how to create ruler guides

- learn how to use guides

- learn how to use color schemes

- learn how to use font schemes

- learn how to create a fill background

- learn how to create an image background.

Page Orientation

Most Publisher templates are designed to be printed on sheets of paper (the exception being the email templates). The default paper size is 21cm x 29.7cm, and is known as A4. The default orientation of the page is portrait, with the shorter sides horizontal and the longer sides vertical. Landscape orientation turns the page so that the page is wider than it is tall.

Try This Yourself:

Open File

Before starting this exercise you MUST open a new, blank publication.

- Click on the Page Design tab, then click on the dialog box launcher for the Page Setup group to display the Page Setup dialog box. The settings shown here are used by Publisher to create new standard, blank publications. Here we can see that the paper size is A4 with portrait orientation...

- Click on [Cancel] to close the dialog box

- On the Page Design tab, click on Orientation in the Page Setup group, then click on Landscape

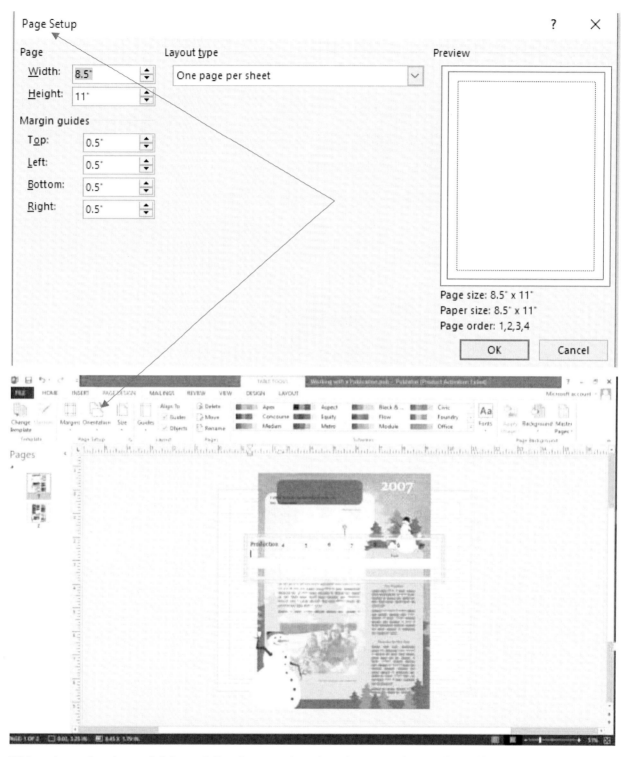

This orientation is useful for publications such as brochures and award certificates

For Your Reference

To change the page orientation:

1. Click on the Page Design tab

2. Click on Orientation in the Page Setup group

3. Click on Landscape or Portrait

• If you think you will need to change the page orientation of your publication, it is advisable to do so before you insert anything or apply any changes – while it is still a blank page. Changing the orientation of a page which has objects on it will cause them to become displaced, forcing you to move them all.

Understanding Page Sizes

Due to the wide range of stationery and print publication choices available, Publisher provides you with a number of page size options for your publications. These options help to ensure that your publication will be printed on the right paper size, whether it be an envelope, a letter, labels, or a poster.

Page Sizes

You can see the full range of paper and page sizes available in Publisher by clicking on More Blank Page Sizes in the Publisher start screen or in the New place on the File tab, or by clicking on the Page Design tab, clicking on Size in the Page Setup group, then selecting More Preset Page Sizes. The More Blank Page Sizes gallery is divided into four sections:

• Standard Page Sizes, which lists all the standard paper sizes on which you can create and ultimately print your publication;

• Custom, which allows you to create your own page size;

• Publication Types, which contains an assortment of blank publication templates; and

• Manufacturers, which provides you with blank publication templates designed to fit stationery from specific manufacturers, such as Post-It N.B..

It is important to remember that the options in Publication Types and Manufacturers are just blank templates; for example, if you choose to make a large banner using a template from the Posters category in Publication Types, it will appear to be one large piece of paper as you are creating it, but it will print over several sheets of A4 paper.

Standard Page Sizes

Publisher allows you to choose from nine different standard paper sizes on which to create your publication: A4, A5, A3, B5, B4, Letter, Executive, Legal, and Tabloid. All of these are available in portrait and landscape orientation. Even if you use a template, your publication will be printed on one of these paper sizes, A4 being the default size. Before printing your publication, ensure that you have paper in the size that you intend to print on, and that your printer is capable of printing on this size.

Publication Types

This section groups a selection of blank templates into categories, such as mailing labels and posters.

This can be useful if you want to create your own publication from scratch, but don't want the hassle of creating the required margins, guidelines, and so on. If you choose a template from this section and use it to create a publication, it will be printed on A4 paper (or other size of your choice) unless a different size is specifically stated. You can also access various stationery manufacturer options in some of the categories.

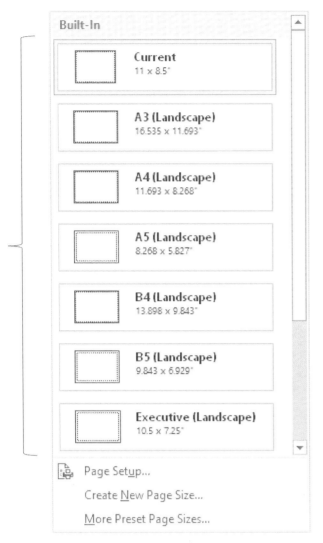

Figure: Different Page sizes

Stationery Manufacturer Templates

Here you can find a range of stationery templates sorted by manufacturer. You might like to use this option if you are creating a publication to be printed by a printing service, or if you have specific stationery which you need to align to. For example, if you are creating a set of mailing labels and you know that your label printer will print them on sheets of labels from Staples, you can select the specific product that you will be printing on so that your publication will be automatically aligned.

Creating Envelopes

You can choose to create envelopes from a publication template or from scratch. The most commonly used envelopes are C6, which is a quarter of an A4 page, and DL, commonly known as a business sized envelope, which is about a third of an A4 page. Once you have an envelope sized publication set up, you can modify it just like any other publication.

Try This Yourself:

Before starting this exercise ensure that a blank publication is displayed...

- Click on the **Page Design tab**

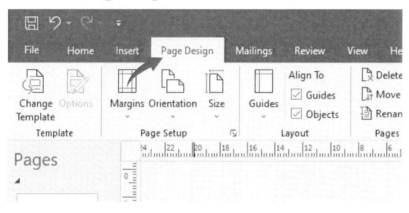

- Click on **Size** in the Page Setup group

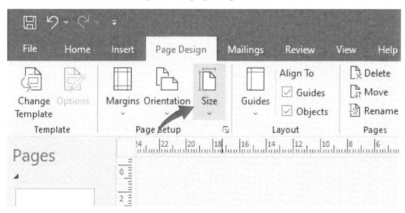

- **Then select More Preset Page Sizes** to display the Preset Page Sizes dialog box

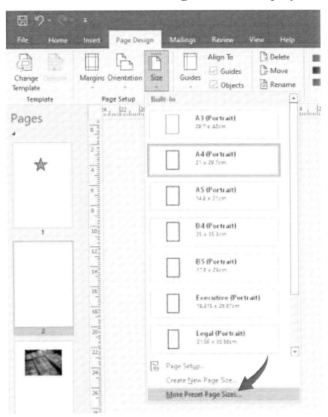

- Click on Envelopes in Publication Types to see a gallery of envelope size options

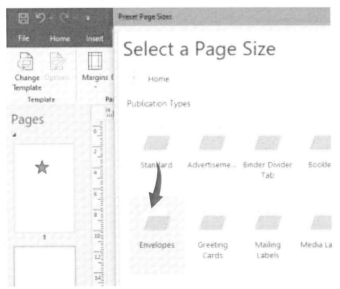

- Click on **DL 22 x 11cm** to select it, then click **on [OK]**

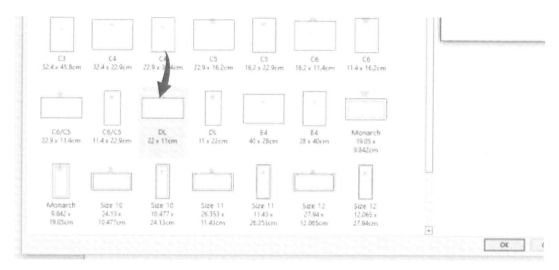

The envelope is now ready for you to add any design elements you like

For Your Reference

To create envelopes:

1. Click on the Page Design tab

2. Click on Size in the Page Setup group, then select More Preset Page Sizes

3. Click on Envelopes in Publication Types

4. Click on the desired envelope size, then click on [OK]

• Before attempting to print envelopes, ensure that your printer is equipped to do so. If it isn't, you may need to get your envelopes printed by a commercial printing service.

Creating Labels

Labels can be created using a publication template or from scratch. The label options in Publisher are designed for Letter paper (8½ x 11 inch) or for A4 paper (21 x 29.7 cm). You must be careful to select label dimensions that match your actual sheets of labels and adjust the side, top and inner margins if necessary.

Try This Yourself:

Before starting this exercise you ensure that a blank publication is displayed...

- Click on the **Page Design tab**

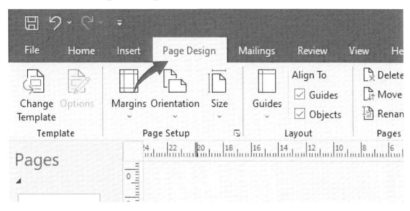

- Click on **Size** in the **Page Setup** group

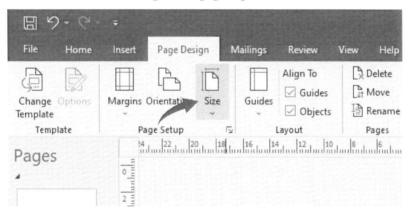

- Select **More Preset Page Sizes** to display the Preset Page Sizes dialog box

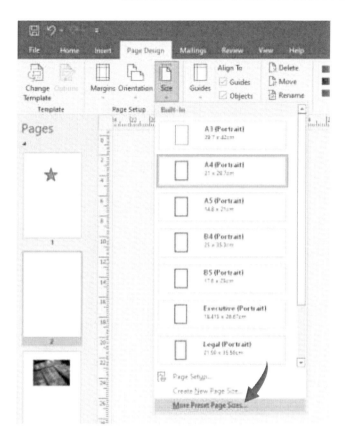

- Click on **Mailing Labels** in Publication Types

- Click on **Avery A4/A5** in Manufacturers

246

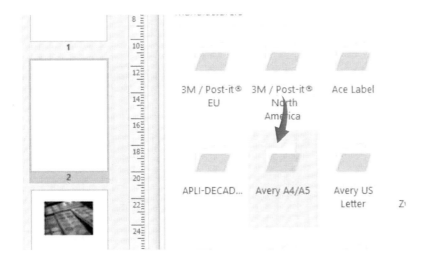

- Scroll to and click on **L7162** to select it

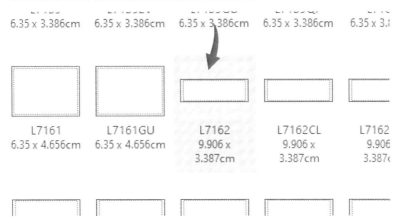

The preview shows us that 16 labels will print on each page…

- Click on [OK] to create the label

For Your Reference

To create labels:

1. Click on the Page Design tab, click on Size in the Page Setup group, then select More Preset Page Sizes

2. Click on Mailing Labels, then click on a Manufacturer

3. Click on a label type, then click on [OK]

• Avery labels prefixed with J or L are designed for A4 paper.

Creating Folded Cards

The Booklet and Folded Card options are used to create books or cards. It is important to remember the difference between publication pages and sheets of paper when making these publications, as one sheet of paper can hold two or four publication pages. When you print the publication, the paper is folded so that the pages are in order.

Try This Yourself:

Before starting this exercise ensure that a blank publication is displayed...

- Click on the **Page Design tab**

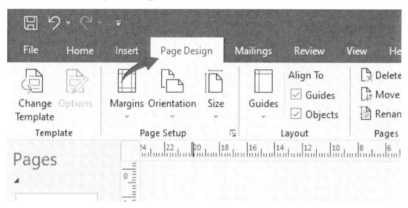

- Click on **Size** in the **Page Setup group**

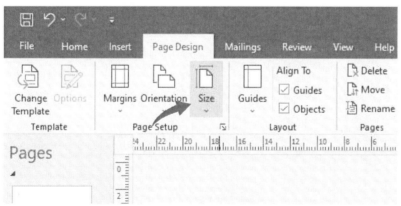

- Select **More Preset Page Sizes** to display the Preset Page Sizes dialog box

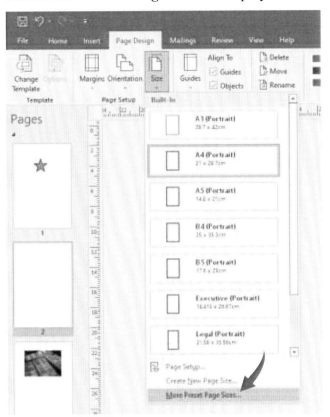

- Click on **Greeting Cards** in Publication Types

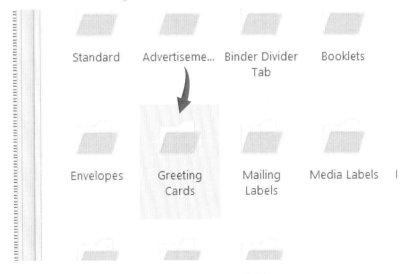

- Click on ¼ **A4 Side Fold 10.5 x 14.8cm** to select it, then click on [OK]

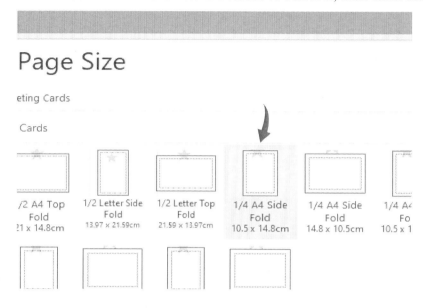

A message will be displayed asking if you want to automatically insert three more pages, as the publication requires four.

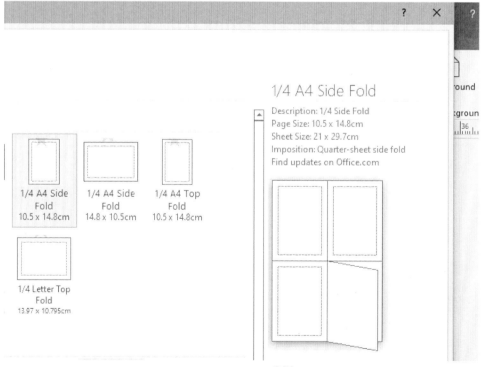

Click on [Yes] to add three more pages to the publication and create a card. Let's see how the card works…

- Click on the **Insert tab**

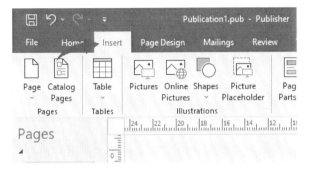

- Click on **Shapes** in the **Illustrations group**

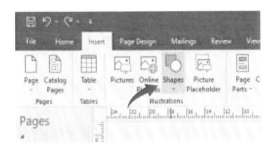

- Click on the **Smiley Face** in Basic Shapes

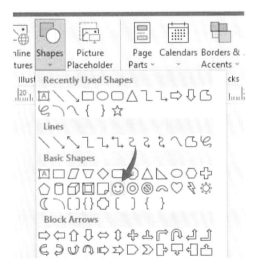

- **Click and drag** to draw the shape as shown

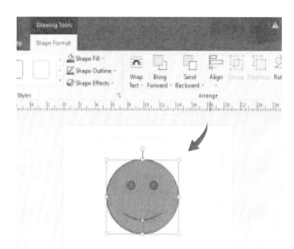

- Click on the **File tab**, then click on **Print** to view a preview of the publication

The first page of the publication only takes up a quarter of an A4 page...

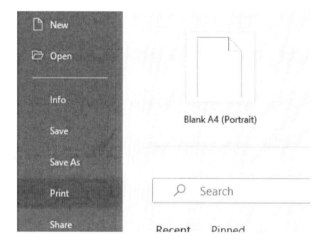

- Press to close the Backstage

For Your Reference.

To create folded cards:

1.   Click on the Page Design tab, click on Size in the Page Setup group, then select More Preset Page Sizes

2.   Click on Greeting Cards in Publication Types, click on a type of card, then click on [OK]

• There are different types of folding cards.

You can choose half or quarter sized pages, as well as choosing between A4 and Letter sized paper.

Changing Margin Guides

The margin guides are the blue lines on the top, bottom and sides of each page in a publication.

These guides allow you to keep a consistent amount of blank space on each side of the page, and allow you to align objects in relation to each other and the page. The margin guides are set to Moderate by default, but you can change them to another preset option or create your own.

Try This Yourself:

Open File

Before starting this exercise you MUST open a new, blank publication.

•   Click on the **Page Design tab**. Let's see what the page looks like with wider margins.

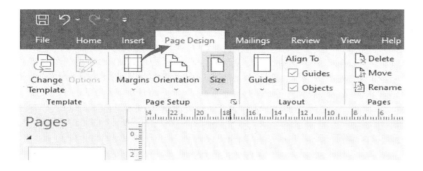

- Click on **Margins** in the Page Setup group, then click on Wide. The margin guides move inward and the margins become bigger. Now let's see what narrow margins look like.

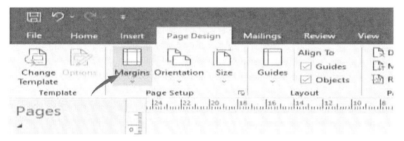

- On the Page Design tab, click on Margins in the Page Setup group, then click on Narrow. The margins move outward.

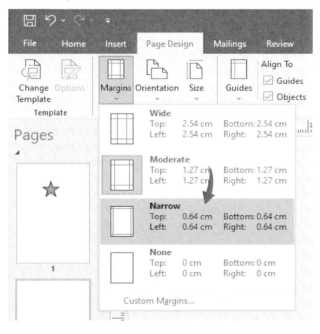

•   Repeat step 3 to click on None. The margin guides move to the very edges of the page. This option is not advisable for a print publication as not all printers are capable of printing to the edges of pages.

•   Repeat step 3 to click on Moderate. The margin guides return to their original positions

For Your Reference

To change the margin guides:

1. Click on the Page Design tab, then click on Margins in the Page Setup group

2. Click on Wide, Narrow, Moderate or None, or Select Custom Margins to create your own

•   The margin guides do not appear on the printed publication.

•   When you drag an object and it aligns with a margin guide, the guide will turn a darker shade of blue until you release the mouse button. This is to help you with alignment.

Creating Grid Guides

Grid guides are used to assist in the placement of objects on the page of a publication. When you create a new publication from scratch there are no layout guides presented other than the margin guides around the page. If you require additional guides, you can create them using Grid Guide settings in the Layout Guides dialog box.

You can create as many guides as you need.

Try This Yourself:

Before starting this exercise ensure that a blank publication is displayed.

•   Click on the **Page Design tab**

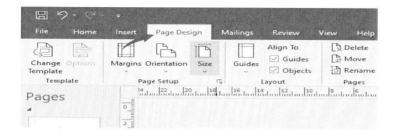

- Click on **Guides** in the **Layout group**

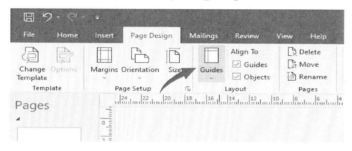

- Select **Grid and Baseline Guides** to display the Layout Guides dialog box. This displays the current guides – grid guides are currently set to one column and one row.

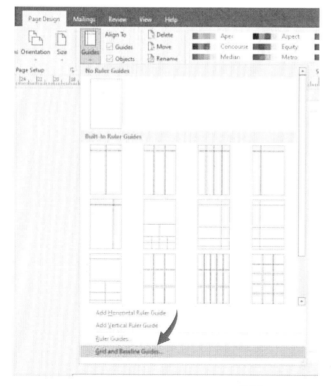

- Click on the up spinner arrow for **Columns** to change the value to **2**

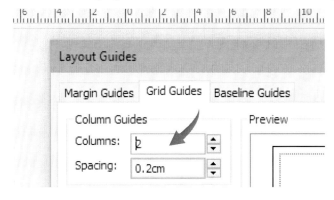

- Click on the up spinner arrow for **Rows** to change the value to **2**

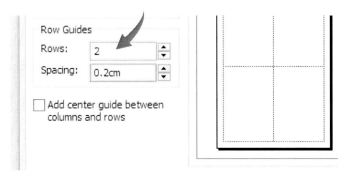

- Click on **[OK]** to apply the new guides to the publication

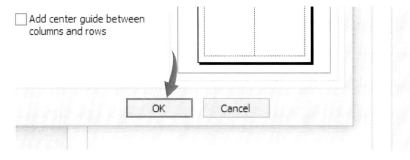

Let's see what happens if we insert another page.

• Click on the Insert tab, then click on the top half of page in the Pages group to insert a new, blank page. The grid guides also appear on this page

For Your Reference

To create grid guides:

1. Click on the **Page Design tab**

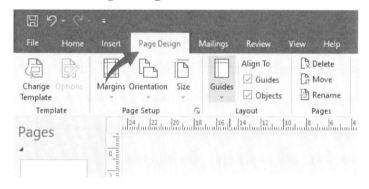

2. Click on **Guides** in the **Layout group**

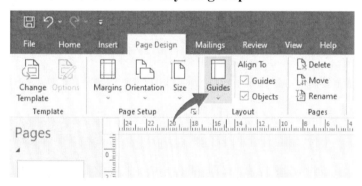

3. Select **Grid and Baseline Guides**

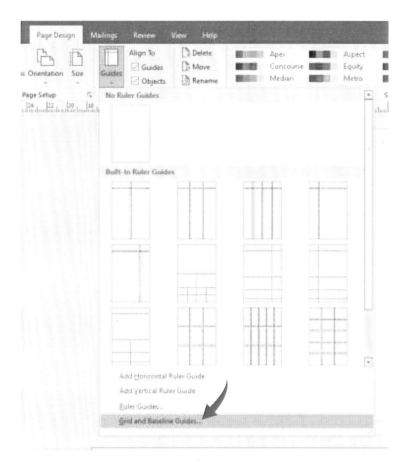

4. Adjust the settings as desired, then click on [OK]

• Grid guides appear on every page in a publication and they can only be moved in the Master Page view. If you only want guides on one page, you might prefer to use ruler guides.

Creating Ruler Guides

Ruler guides are similar to grid guides in that they are guidelines on the page which help you to align design elements. However, ruler guides are green instead of blue, are only inserted on one page, and can easily be moved. You can insert ruler guides from the Page Design tab, or by clicking and dragging the rulers at the left and top of the publication window.

Try This Yourself:

Open File

Before starting this exercise you MUST open a new, blank publication.

- Click on the **Page Design tab**

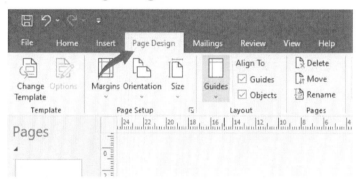

- Then click on **Guides** in the Layout group. A menu of ruler guide options is displayed

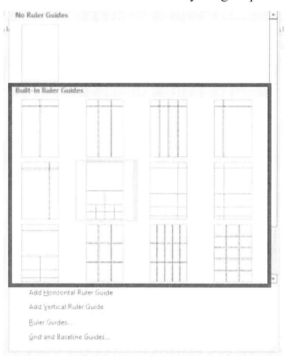

- Click on 3 Columns with Heading, the **second option in the first row**. The ruler guides are applied to the page.

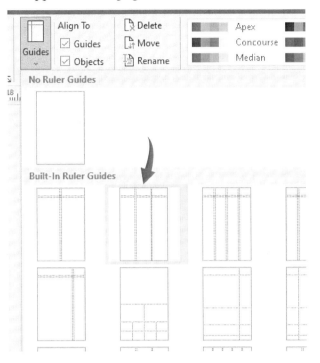

- Point to the top horizontal ruler guide until the mouse pointer changes to a double headed arrow, then click and drag it up, as shown. Let's insert a ruler guide another way.

- Point to the ruler to the left of the publication window until the mouse pointer changes to a double headed arrow

- Click and drag to the right to create a ruler guide, then drag it onto the page, as shown.

For Your Reference

To create ruler guides:

- Click on the Page Design tab, click on Guides in the Layout group, then select a preset option, or

- Point to one of the rulers in the publication window, then click and drag onto the page

- Unlike grid guides, ruler guides only appear on the page on which they were inserted.

Using Guides

Once you have learned how to insert guides, you need to know how to use them. Guides are used to align objects to each other as well as to different points on the page. They will only be activated if you move objects by dragging them with the mouse; you cannot use the guides while nudging objects using the arrow keys.

Try This Yourself:

Open File

Before starting this exercise you MUST open the file Design And Layout_1.pub…

•   Select the text box closest to the bottom of the page. This text box contains information regarding times and prices for the exhibition…

•   Drag the text box down and to the left, so that the text box is centered horizontally on the page and the top of the text box aligns with the bottom grid guide, as shown.

A pink guideline will appear down the centre of the page when the text box is centered.

•   Click and drag the pictures to align them, as shown

•   Select the text box containing the text. Featuring major projects, drag it to align it to the centre of the page, then align it to the bottom of the top grid guide

•   Click and drag the WordArt heading and the text box at the top of the page to align them to the centre of the page, as shown

For Your Reference

To align objects to guides:

1. Select the object

2. Drag it to the desired guide until the guide is activated

• Pink guides only appear in certain situations, such as when the edges of two objects are aligned, or when an object is aligned to the centre of the page.

Using Color Schemes

Publisher provides you with a selection of color schemes to choose from when creating your publication. Each color scheme consists of eight complementary colors, which are automatically applied to different elements of your publication. Different color schemes are appropriate for different situations – some color schemes are quite subtle, while others are very bright.

For Your Reference

To change the color scheme:

1. Click on the **Page Design tab**

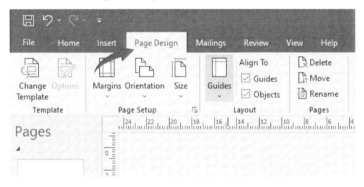

2. Click on the **More arrow** for Color Schemes in the **Schemes group**

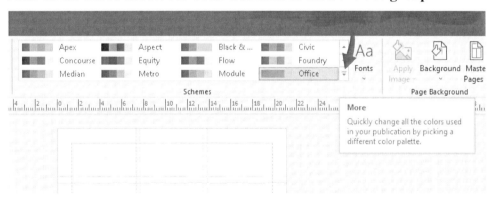

3. Select a **color scheme**

•   You can preview different color schemes using Live Preview – simply point to a color scheme in the gallery without selecting it

•   You can create your own color scheme. After clicking on the More arrow for the Color Schemes gallery, select Create New Color Scheme.

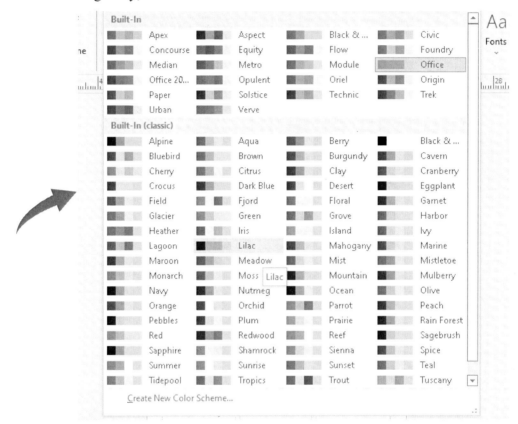

Using Font Schemes

Similar to the color schemes, Publisher provides you with groups of fonts which work well together.

These groups of fonts are known as Font Schemes. Each font scheme features a heading font, which will be applied to the headings in the publication, and a body font, which will be applied to the rest of the text.

Try This Yourself:

Same File

Continue using the previous file with this exercise, or open the file Design And Layout_3.pub.

- Click on the **Page Design tab**

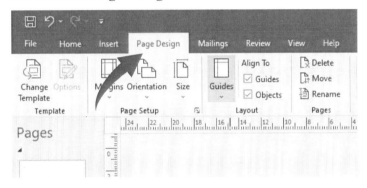

- Then click on **Fonts** in the **Schemes group** to display a gallery of options.

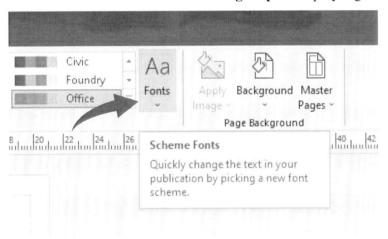

• Click on **Calligraphy** under **Built-In** to apply this font scheme to the publication. This font scheme uses a font which is small by default. We could make all the text bigger, but we'll change to a different font scheme instead.

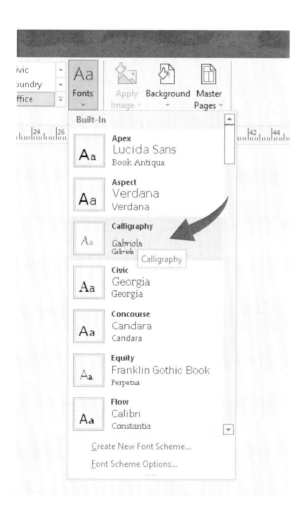

• Repeat step 1, then scroll to and click on Casual under Built-In (classic) to apply this font scheme. Let's find a more appropriate font scheme for this publication.

• Repeat step 1, then scroll to and click on Offset under Built-In (classic) to apply this font scheme

For Your Reference

To change the font scheme:

1. Click on the Page Design tab

2. Click on Font in the Schemes group

3. Select a font scheme

• As with color schemes, you can view font schemes in Live Preview and create your own font scheme. You might find this useful if you create several publications and need to consistently use the same fonts.

Creating A Fill Background

There may be times when you want to create a background for your publication, perhaps to make it stand out more or to make it more interesting to look at. A basic, subtle background, such as a fill or a pattern, can enhance your publication without distracting the reader from the information you are trying to convey.

Try This Yourself:

Open File

Before starting this exercise you MUST open the file Design And Layout_4.pub.

• Click on the **Page Design tab**

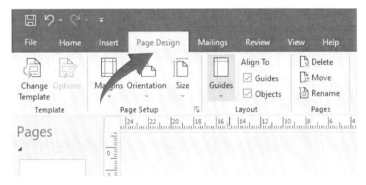

- Then click on **Background** in the **Page Background group** to display a gallery of options

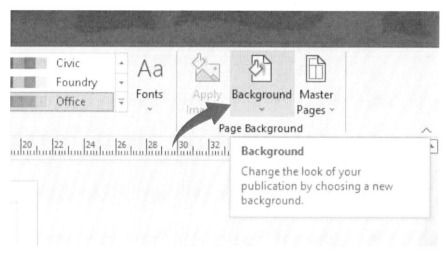

- Click on **30% tint of Accent 2**, the second option in the second row under Solid Background

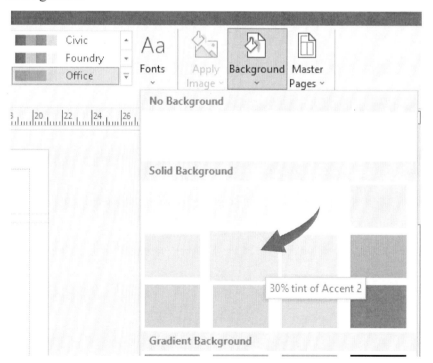

Let's find something a little more interesting.

- Repeat step 1, then select More Backgrounds to display the Format Background pane
- Click on **Pattern fill** to select it, then click on the Solid diamond pattern, as shown

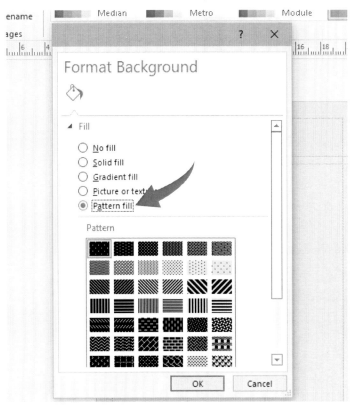

- Click on the drop arrow for the **Foreground color**, then select **Hyperlink (RGB (51,153,0)), Lighter 80%,** the sixth option in the second row
- Click on the drop arrow for the Background color, then select Accent 3 (RGB (214, 224, 214)), the fourth option in the top row
- Click on [OK] to apply the background

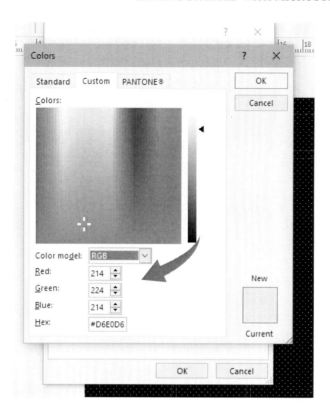

For Your Reference

To create a fill background:

1. Click on the Page Design tab, then click on Background in the Page Background group

2. Select an option, or Select More Backgrounds, select the desired options, and then click on [OK]

• When creating a fill background, be careful not to use a color or pattern that will overpower the rest of your publication. A background that is too bright or too eye-catching can distract the reader or make the text difficult to read.

Creating An Image Background

Fills and patterns aren't your only options for backgrounds – you can also choose to use an image.

After choosing an image, you can set its transparency before applying it to the publication. The higher the transparency, the more washed-out the image will appear. This can help you to ensure that the background image doesn't overpower the rest of the publication.

Try This Yourself:

Same File

Continue using the previous file with this exercise, or open the file Design And Layout_5.pub.

- Click on the **Page Design tab**

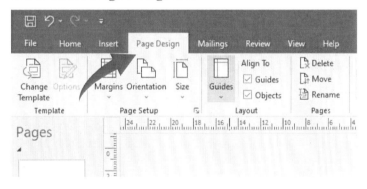

- Click on **Background** in the **Page Background group**

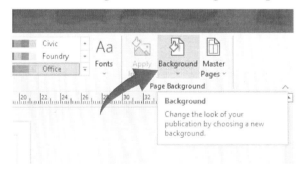

- Then select **More Backgrounds** to display the Format Background pane

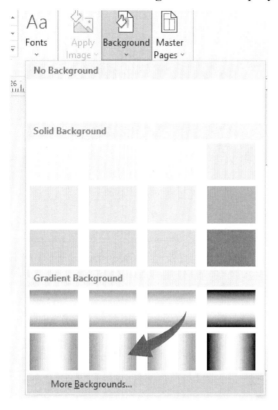

- Click on **Picture** or **texture fill** to select it

- Under **Insert picture from**, click on **[Online]** to display the Insert Pictures pane

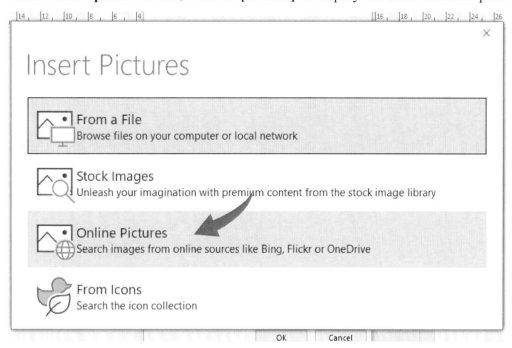

- Click in the search box for Bing Image Search, type **golf**, then press

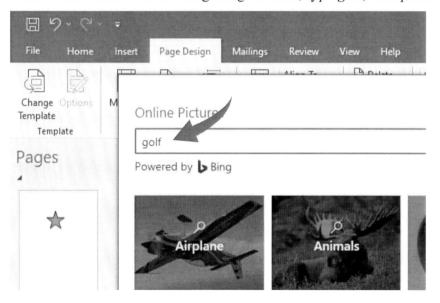

Click on the first image to select it, then click on [Insert]

- Click and drag the slider for Transparency to set it to 85%
- Click on [OK] to apply the new background

For Your Reference

To create an image background:

1. Click on the Page Design tab, click on Background in the Page Background group, then select More Backgrounds

2. Click on Picture or texture fill

3. Click on the location from which to insert the picture

4. Navigate to the desired picture, select it, then click on [Insert]

5. Set the transparency as desired

6. Click on [OK].

Chapter 11

Master Pages!

INFOCUS

Master pages are a useful tool for creating and working with large publications, where maintaining consistency over multiple pages is important. A master page can be used to apply design and layout elements to multiple pages at once which can save you the time and effort of applying these elements individually to every page.

In this session you will:

- gain an understanding of master pages

- learn how to use a master page

- learn how to insert headers

- learn how to insert footers

- learn how to insert page numbers

- learn how to use a two page master

- learn how to create additional master pages

- learn how to use multiple master pages.

Understanding Master Pages

You can access the Master Page view by clicking on the View tab, then clicking on Master Page in the Views group. Using the Master Page view, you can quickly and easily make changes to your whole publication by applying elements to some or all of the pages at the same time.

Master Pages

A master page is a page that is attached to a publication but doesn't appear within the publication itself. By default, all publications (including blank publications) contain a master page. In order to view the master page for your publication you must access Master Page view.

Any changes you make to a master page are applied to all pages within that publication to which that master page is applied. You can therefore use master pages to apply design elements such as headers, footers, page numbers, headings, text, and pictures to multiple pages within a publication. These elements then become part of the background of the pages in the publication and can only be edited using the master page. Keep in mind that when working with a master page, if you want elements to appear on some pages but not others, you will either need to choose to apply no master page to some pages, create a second master page, or apply the elements to each page individually. If you decide that you would prefer to add content and design elements to each page individually, then you don't have to use a master page at all; you can simply leave the master page blank.

The Master Page View

The Master Page view is activated when you:

- Click on the View Tab

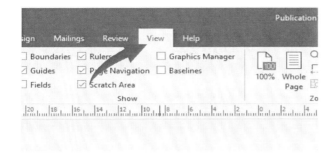

- Click on **Master Page**.

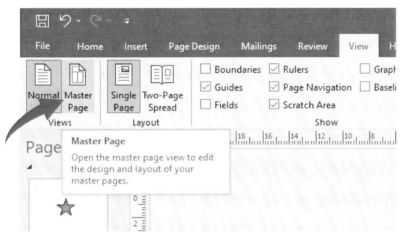

- You can also access the Master Page by clicking on the **Page Design tab**

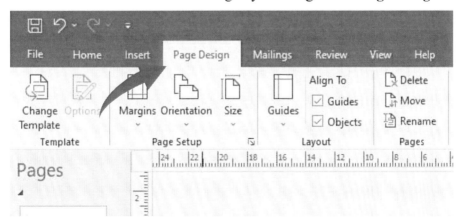

- Clicking on Master Pages in the Page Background group

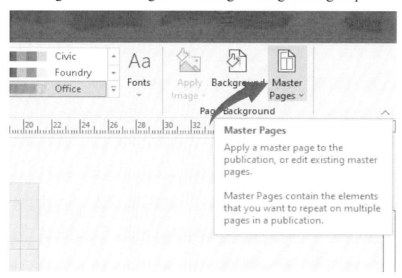

- Then selecting **Edit Master Pages,** or by clicking on the Insert tab, then clicking on Header or Footer in the Header & Footer group.

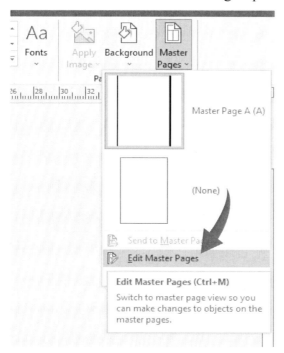

When a publication is in Master Page view, the normal pages of the publication are not displayed.

Rather, the master page will appear in the publication window, and the Pages navigation pane will display thumbnail previews of each master page in the publication. The area surrounding the page in the publication window will change color from grey to yellow and the Master Page tab will appear on the ribbon, as shown below. This tab is only accessible in Master Page view and provides you with a range of commands for working with master pages.

Using Master Pages

You can use master pages to ensure your publication is consistently based on the same layout and design elements throughout. This can not only save you time and effort, but also ensure that your final publication looks professional and serves its purpose effectively.

As useful as master pages are, there will be times when you will find that it is not appropriate to use them in a publication; for example, when using some templates. Because master page elements become part of the background of the pages in a publication, all other content applied to the pages is inserted over the top. When using a template, you may find that elements that you placed on the master page are obscured in the publication by objects from the template. As you cannot set content to be placed behind the background, you would be better off applying the elements from the master page to each page of the publication individually to ensure they are visible in this situation.

Using A Master Page

If you have one master page in a publication, anything you insert on that master page will then appear in the background of every normal page in that publication, unless you specify otherwise.

You can also choose to send an item from a normal page to a master page so that an element which initially only appeared on one page can appear in the same place on every page (such as a logo).

Try This Yourself:

Open File

Before starting this exercise you MUST open the file Master Pages_1.pub...

- Click on the **View tab**

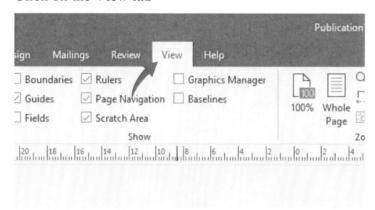

- Then click on **Master Page** in the Views group to display the publication in Master Page view. The Master Page is blank…

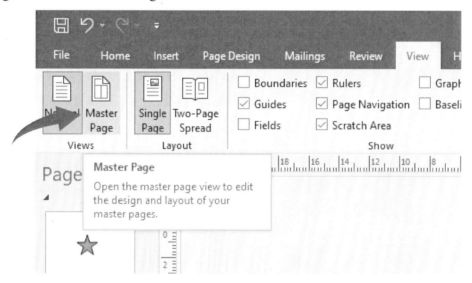

- Click on the **Page Design tab**

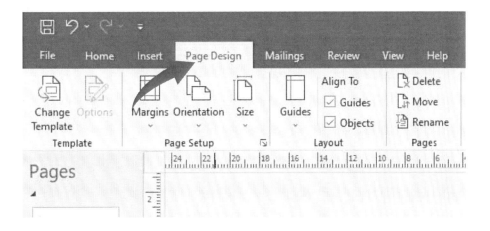

- Click on **Background** in the Page Background group

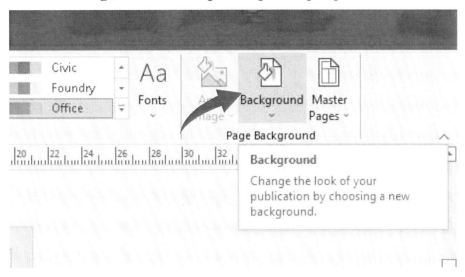

- Then **click on 30% tint of Accent 2**, the second option in the second row under Solid Background

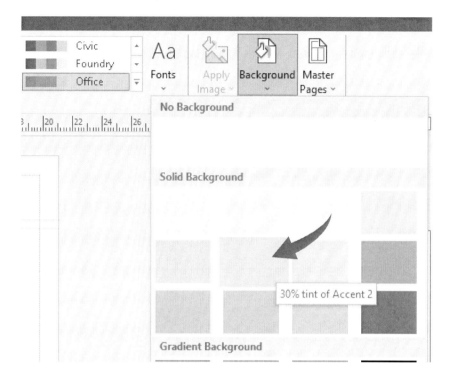

• Click on the Master Page tab, then click on Close Master Page in the Close group. The background is applied to every page. Let's send the logo to the master page right corner of the first page

• Click on the **Page Design tab**, click on Master Pages in the Page Background group, then select Send to Master Page. A message is displayed confirming the object was sent.

• Click on [OK], then click on Page 2 in the Pages navigation pane to see the logo on this page

For Your Reference

To use a master page:

1. Click on the View tab, then click on Master Page in the Views group

2. Insert or apply the desired elements to the master page

3. Click on the Master Page tab, then click on Close Master Page in the Close group

• When your publication is in Master Page view, the Pages navigation pane displays thumbnail previews of each of your master pages. Instead of being numbered 1, 2, 3, and so on, the master pages are labelled A, B, C, etc.

Inserting Headers

Traditionally, a header is an object that appears at the top of every page. In Publisher, headers are created on the master page. They appear on every page, but can only be modified when the master page is displayed. Headers can include text, page numbers, date and time stamps, and graphics.

Try This Yourself:

Same File

Continue using the previous file with this exercise, or open the file Master Pages_2.pub...

• Click on page 1 in the Pages navigation pane to display the first page of the publication

• Click on the **Insert tab**

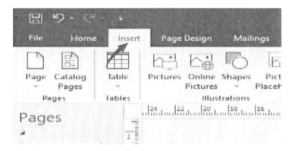

• Then click on **Header** in the **Header & Footer group**. The publication will switch to Master Page view, with the text insertion point in the header area of the master page.

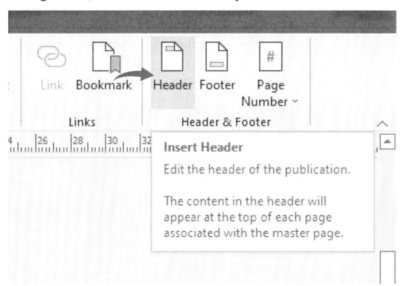

- On the **Master Page tab**

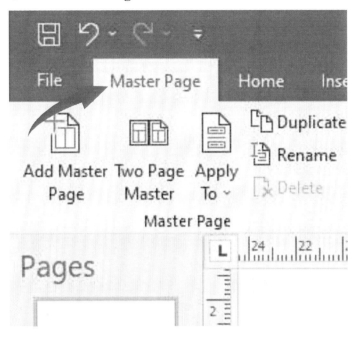

- Click on **Insert Date** in the Header & Footer group. Today's date will be inserted after the text.

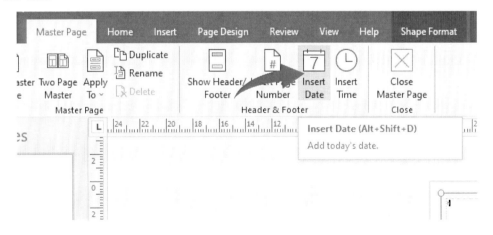

- On the **Master Page tab**, click on **Close Master Page** in the Close group to return the publication to Normal view.

Notice that the header appears on every page

For Your Reference

To insert a header:

1. Click on the Insert tab, then click on Header in the Header & Footer group

2. Type or insert the desired information

3. Click on the Master Page tab, then click on Close Master Page in the Close group

• You can format the text of headers and footers just as you can format ordinary text by changing the font, size, style and alignment.

Inserting Footers

While a header appears at the top of every page, a footer appears at the bottom. Footers often include information such as page numbers, company names and taglines. Like headers, footers are inserted on the master page and will appear on every page that the master page is applied to.

Try This Yourself:

Same File

Continue using the previous file with this exercise, or open the file Master Pages_3.pub.

- Click on the **View tab**

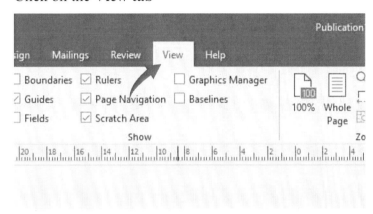

- Then click on **Master Page** in the **Views group**. The publication will switch to Master Page view.

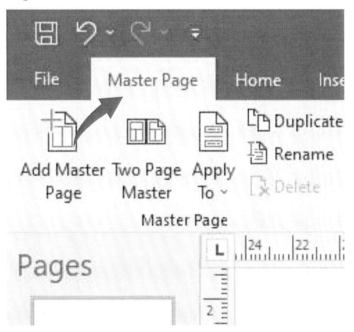

- On the Master Page tab, click twice **on Show Header/Footer** in the Header & Footer group to open the footer area of the master page.

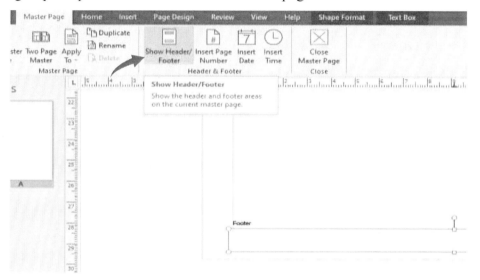

- Type **Greening the Globe**

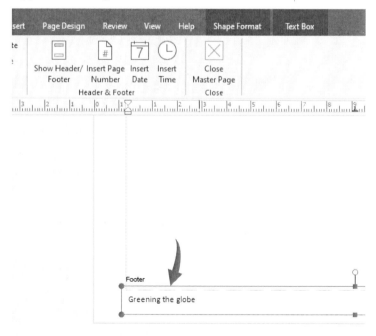

• On the Master Page tab, click on Close Master Page in the Close group to return the publication to Normal view. The footer is inserted on every page.

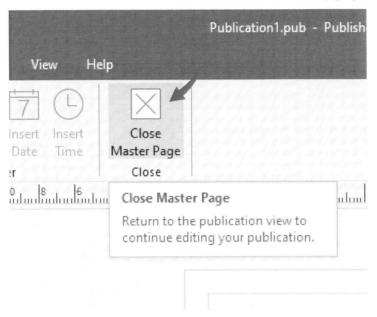

For Your Reference

To insert a footer:

1. Click on the Insert tab, then click on Footer in the Header & Footer group

2. Type or insert the desired information

3. Click on the Master Page tab, then click on Close Master Page in the Close group

• Page numbers can be inserted into headers and footers. They can be aligned to the left, right or centre.

Inserting Page Numbers

Page numbers are common in print publications and are especially useful in a publication with many pages. In Publisher, page numbers can be inserted into the header or footer of a master page where they appear as a hash symbol (#).

When the publication is returned to Normal view, the symbol will become a number corresponding to the position of the page in the publication.

Try This Yourself:

Same File

Continue using the previous file with this exercise, or open the file Master Pages_4.pub.

- Click on the View tab

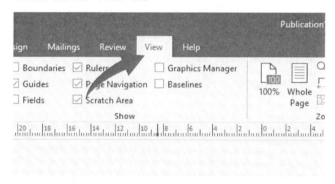

- Then click on Master Page in the Views group

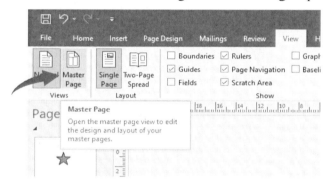

- On the Master Page tab, click twice on Show Header/Footer in the Header & Footer group to open the footer for editing

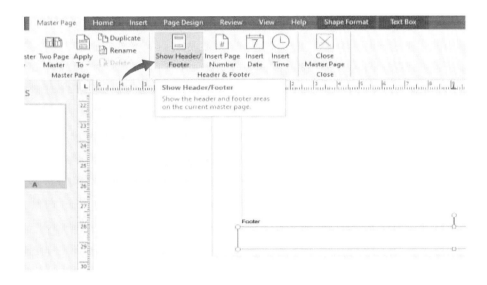

• Click at the end of the word Globe in the footer, then press twice to move the insertion point to the right end of the footer

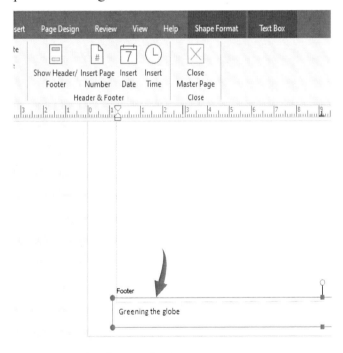

• Type Page, then press

- On the Master Page tab, click on Insert Page Number in the Header & Footer group. A hash symbol (#) is inserted.

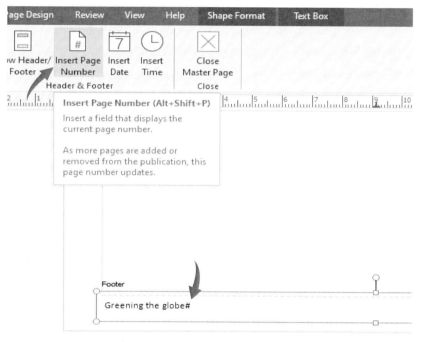

- On the Master Page tab, click on Close Master Page in the Close group to return the publication to Normal view

Each page now has a number

For Your Reference

To insert page numbers:

1. Click on the View tab, then click on Master Page in the Views group

2. Click in the header or footer

3. On the Master Page tab, click on Insert Page Number in the Header & Footer group

• You can insert page numbers without going into Master Page view. Simply click on the Insert tab, click on Page Number in the Header & Footer group, then select the position on the page to insert the numbers. Be aware that this method will affect any headers or footers already applied.

Using A Two Page Master

Many publications are designed to be viewed as a booklet or two-page spread. In this situation you might prefer to use a Two Page Master. A two page master allows you to specify what appears on the left and right pages of a two page spread. Note that switching from a single master page to a two page master will cause some elements to be mirrored on the left master page.

Try This Yourself:

Same File

Continue using the previous file with this exercise, or open the file Master Pages_5.pub.

•   Click on the View tab

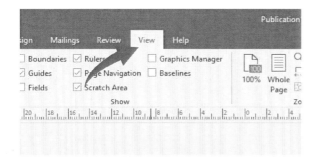

- Then click on Master Page in the Views group

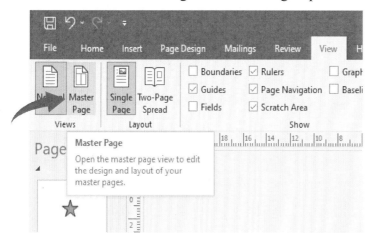

- On the Master Page tab, click on **Two Page Master** in the Master Page group to switch to a two page master. The former single master page becomes the right page of the two page master, and the logo is mirrored on the new left page.

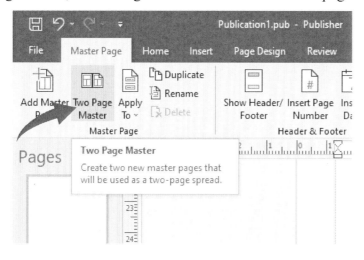

- On the Master Page tab, click on **Close Master Page** in the Close group to return to Normal view

- Click on page 2 in the Pages navigation pane to display it. This page would be on the left in a two-page spread and so the left page of the two page master has been applied.

- Click on the View tab, then click on Two-Page Spread in the Layout group to view the publication as a two-page spread

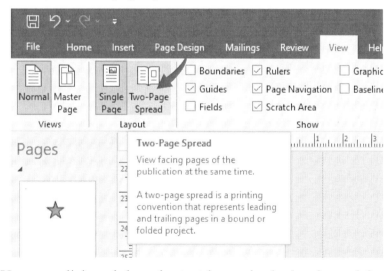

Note: You can click and drag the text boxes in the header and footer areas to ensure they align.

For Your Reference

To use a two page master:

1. Click on the View tab, then click on Master Page in the Views group

2. On the Master Page tab, click on Two Page Master

• When you switch from a single master page to a two page master, any elements (aside from headers and footers) already on the single page will be mirrored in the new one.

This includes images, guidelines and text boxes; however, the text inside the text boxes will not be mirrored.

Creating Additional Master Pages

There may be times when you want to apply certain design and layout elements to different pages. In this situation you can create multiple master pages, and choose which one to apply to each page of your publication. For example, a brochure with many topics and pages might have one master page for each topic title page, and another for the content pages.

Try This Yourself:

Same File

Continue using the previous file with this exercise, or open the file Master Pages_6.pub.

•   Click on the View tab

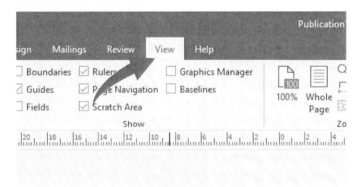

•   Then click on Master Page in the Views group to switch to Master Page view. Let's create a new master page.

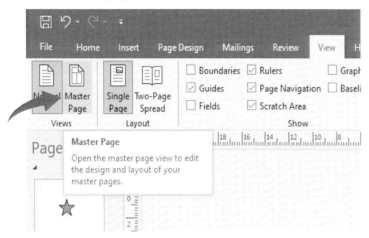

•   On the Master Page tab, click on **Add Master Page** in the Master Page group to display the New Master Page dialog box

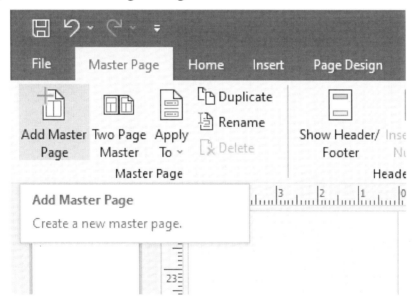

•   Click on Two-page master so it appears unticked

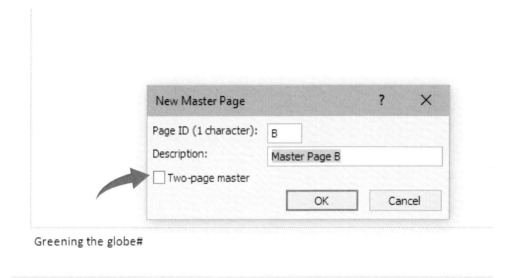

Greening the globe#

- Click on [OK] to create the new master page

- Click on the Page Design tab, click on Background in the Page Background group, then click on 30% tint of Accent 2 under Solid Background to apply this background

- Click on the Master Page tab, then click on Close Master Page in the Close group to return to Normal view

For Your Reference

To create an additional master page:

1. Click on the View tab, then click on Master Page in the Views group

2. On the Master Page tab, click on Add Master Page in the Master Page group

3. Set the options as desired, then click on [OK]

• When you create new master pages, they will not be applied to any of the pages of your publication until you specify otherwise.

Using Multiple Master Pages

When you have a publication with more than one master page, you can choose which master page to apply to each normal page in the publication.

You also have the option of applying no master page to a publication page. You can choose these specifications in both Normal view and Master Page view.

Try This Yourself:

Same File

Continue using the previous file with this exercise, or open the file Master Pages_7.pub.

*   Click on the View tab

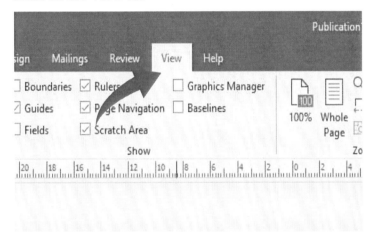

*   Then click on Master Page in the Views group to switch the publication to Master Page view

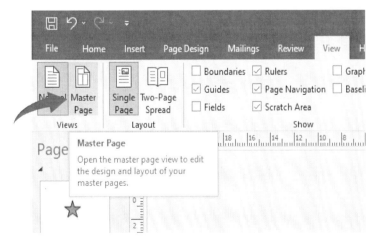

- Click on master page in the Pages navigation pane to display the second master page
- On the Master Page tab, click on **Apply To** in the Master Page group, then select Apply Master Page to display the Apply Master Page dialog box

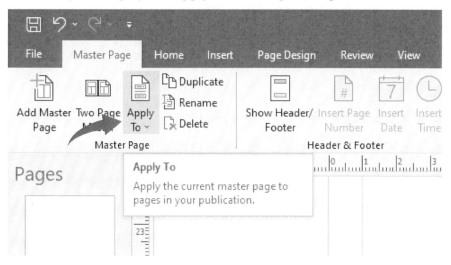

- Click on Pages to select it, then type 1 in to, as shown
- Click on [OK] to apply master page B to the first page of the publication

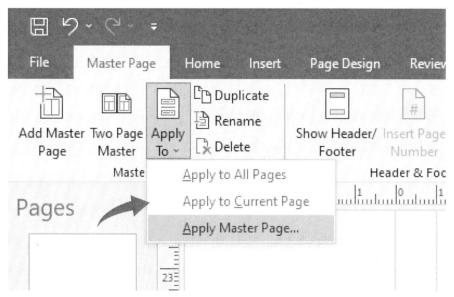

• On the Master Page tab, click on Close Master Page in the Close group to return to Normal view

• Click on page 4 in the Pages navigation pane to display the last page of the publication

• Click on the Page Design tab, click on Master Pages in the Page Background group, then select (None) to apply neither of the master pages to this page

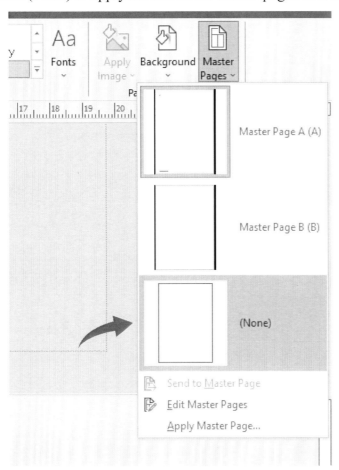

For Your Reference

To apply a master page:

1. Click on the View tab, then click on Master Page in the Views group

2. Select the desired master page

3. On the Master Page tab, click on Apply To in the Master Page group, then select the desired

option

To apply no master pages to a page:

1. Select the publication page

2. Click on the Page Design tab, then click on Master Pages in the Page Background group

3. Select (None).

Chapter 12

Publisher Mail Merge!

In This Chapter

- All About Publisher Mail Merge
- Creating a Data Source
- Creating a Mail Merge Publication
- Showing Merge Results
- Sorting a Merge
- Filtering Data
- Merge Printing
- Clearing a Filter

INFOCUS

What is the Publisher Mail Merge Feature?

Combining a publication with specific information for multiple people and/or companies is known as mail merging. You might create a series of address labels or one-of-a-kind mailings for a list of people.

To create a mail merge, you need a publication and a list of the recipients' names and addresses. The publisher sends a copy of the letter or publication to each person and address on the list.

Each copy of the publication will include sensitive data belonging to one of your recipients. This is a great way to save time and money when you need to convey the same information to several people.

In this session you will:

*   learn how to create a mail merge data source

*   learn how to create a mail merge publication

*   learn how to show the results of a merge

*   learn how to sort a merge

*   learn how to filter merge data

*   learn how to print the results of a merge

*   learn how to clear a filter.

Creating A Data Source

A data source is necessary for every mail combine.

The names and addresses of your consumers must be entered into a data source that the primary merge publication refers to, for instance, if you want to send a customised pricing list to each of your clients.

The best way to think of data sources is as rows and columns of information organized into tables.

Put This to the Test:

File Opening

It is ESSENTIAL that you OPEN the file Mail Merge 1.pub before beginning this practice.

- Click on the Mailings tab

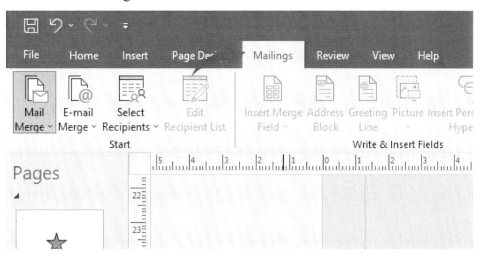

- Click on Select Recipients in the Start group

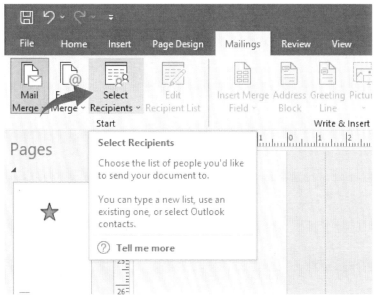

- Then select. Type a New List to display the New Address List dialog box

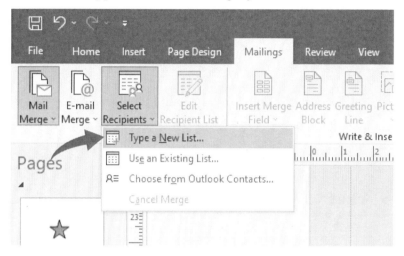

- Press to change the insertion point to First Name after typing Ms in Title. Fill out the remaining fields as directed, pushing to advance to the next field after each entry. Type Kelly, press, then type Long in the Last Name field.

- New Melbourne Light Orchestra, Melbourne, VIC, 3000, GPO Box 453

Click [New Entry] to start a new record after repeating steps 2 through 5 to make a total of six more entries, as shown by Name Address. To open the Save Address List dialog box, click [OK].

Mrs. Carol Nhan Music Mania Sydney NSW 2004 220 High St Thespian Mr. Joe Watts 29 Marigold St. Adelaide SA 5030 Ms. Diva Sposito,

After navigating to the course files folder, type "Customers" in the File name field and click [Save]. Australia's Arts Industry Association, Sydney, 2004 Sini Ivanovich

The Mail Merge Recipients dialog box contains a list of the customers.

Kinetic Dance Energy 2/258 Seaview St., Cottesloe, WA 6023

Miss Sarla Tariq

• Click [OK] after making sure each name is ticked.

Stellar SciFi Club, 10 Amess St., Carlton, Victoria, 3054 Nancy Buckley

Albury, NSW 2657, 5 Evans St. Ibsen Society of Henrik

For Your Information

Making a merge data source entails:

1. From the Select Recipients option in the Start group of the Mailings tab, choose Type a New List.

2. Click [OK] after inputting each data record.

3. Name the database, pick a place for it to be saved, and then click [Save].

For Publisher, a data source file is not a publishing file. If a data source file has the.mdb file extension, Microsoft Access is compatible with it. You can change the data in Microsoft Access, copy it to Microsoft Word, or do both if necessary.

Mail Merge Publication Creation

Any publication may be used for merging. The sole actual requirement is that it must be adaptable in some way so that it may be produced repeatedly utilizing the data from the data source.

A mail merge publication differs from other publications in that it contains field codes that indicate where the data from the data source will be put.

Put This to the Test:

Equal File

When Publisher prompts you to validate the data source file when you open a merging publication that was previously linked to a data source, select [Yes] if the listed source file is accurate and you wish to keep the link.

• To open the Mail Merge task pane, pick Step-by-Step Mail Merge Wizard from the Start group's Mail

- Merge drop-down menu by clicking the Mailings tab's bottom half. The recipient list for this merging publication is automatically chosen from the previously prepared customer list. Inserting merge fields into the publication, which will control where the content is put, is our first step.

- To prevent this option from being selected, click Preview Results in the Preview Results group on the Mailings tab.

- Click the publication's "This certificate entitles" link, then click

- Repeat step 4 to enter the First Name and Last Name fields, type of, press, then insert the City field.

For your reference

Click on Title in the Mail Merge task pane to input the merge field.

Developing a combine publication

1. Select Step-by-Step Mail Merge Wizard from the Start group by clicking the Mailings tab's bottom half of the Mail Merge menu.

2. Place the insertion point, then click to add merge fields.

• At the bottom of the Mail Merge task pane, click Previous: Create recipient list if you wish to use a different recipient list for your mail merge.

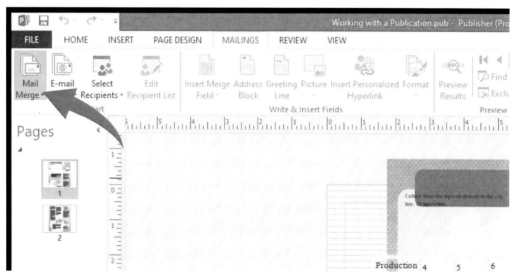

SHOWING MERGE RESULTS

You may preview the data in the publication to see how it will look after your data source and merging publication are linked. The merging results can be shown immediately on the screen or printed. When you execute a merging to the screen, you may move through the records and evaluate each publication individually to make sure it all looks the way you expected it to.

Put This to the Test:

• Open the file Mail Merge 3.pub to continue with this practice using the previous file.

• To examine information about the first recipient, select the Mailings tab and then click Preview Results in the Preview Results group.

• To examine the following combined record, select Next in Preview recipient from the Mail Merge task pane.

• For each record, repeat step 2 to view it.

• To get back to the first record, click First in Preview recipient.

For Your Information

To display the merge's outcomes:

1.   Select the Mailings tab, then select Preview Results from the group under Preview Results.

2.   To navigate between entries in the Mail Merge task window, click on the arrows next to Preview recipient.

• When you open or save a publication, the results of the merge are instantly presented.

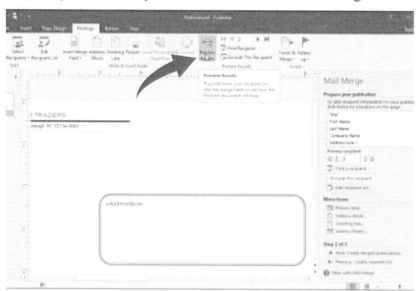

Sorting A Merge

Merged records are shown in the data source's order of placement unless you specify otherwise. The sequence in which the records were entered is typically the only organization for the data source. Your merging may be organized in a variety of ways by sorting. You may, for instance, arrange the data source according to client name or city.

You Can Try This:

- To see the Mail Merge Recipients dialog box, choose Edit recipient list in the Mail Merge task pane.

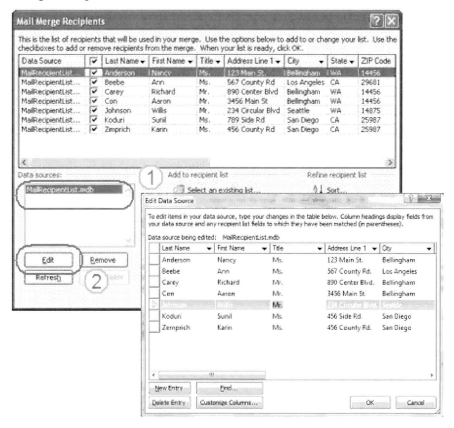

- To access the Sort Records pane of the Filter and Sort dialog box, choose Sort from the Refine recipient list option.

- Scroll to City and choose it by clicking the arrow next to Sort by.

- Click on the drop-down arrow next to Then by and choose Last Name. A second level sort is created based on last name within a city.

- Click [OK] to view the results in the Mail Merge Recipients dialog box. Sydney is classified as the final city, and Ms. Nhan is mentioned before Ms. Sposito there. Adelaide is listed as the first city.

- Click [OK] to save the changes to the publication.

- In the recipient preview, click Next to explore each record in detail. The records are now organized by city, then by last name.

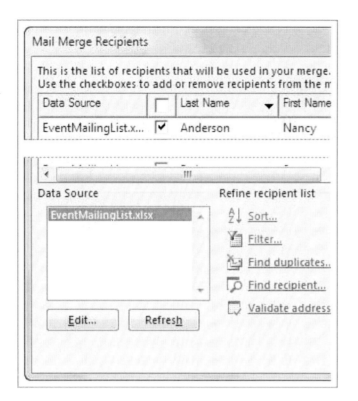

For Your Reference

To sort a merge:

1. Click on Edit recipient list in the Mail Merge task pane

2. Click on Sort

3. Select the field/s to sort the records by

4. Click on [OK], then click on [OK] again

• When conducting a merge, you can change to a descending sort (Z to A) by clicking on Descending in the Filter and Sort dialog box.

• You can click on Edit Recipient List in the Start group on the Mailings tab to conduct a sort.

Filtering Data

It's possible that you won't always wish to make publications for every recipient in the list of data sources. For instance, you could want to provide a special price list to customers in a certain suburb. To do this, data in the source file can be filtered. The three elements of a filter are the field to be filtered by, the comparison operator, and the example to search for.

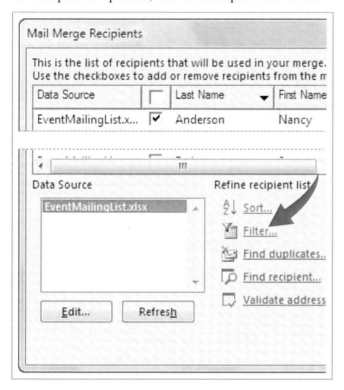

- Try It Yourself with the Same File

- Open the file Mail Merge 5.pub to continue with this practice using the preceding file.

- To see the Mail Merge Recipients dialog box, select Edit recipient list in the Mail Merge task pane.

- To see the Filter Records tab of the Filter and Sort dialog box, click Filter under Refine recipient list.

- Select Field by clicking the drop-down arrow, then scroll to and select State.

- Select Compare to, then enter NSW.

- The Equal to comparison value guarantees that Publisher only combines data whose State is NSW.

- To return to the merging publication, click [OK], then [OK] again.

- To examine each filtered record, click Next in the Mail Merge task pane's Preview recipient

For Your Information

To sort combined records:

1. In the Mail Merge task pane, choose Edit recipient list, then select Filter.

2. After choosing the fields to filter for, enter the filter criteria.

3. Select [OK], then select [OK] once more.

• The 'or' and 'and' operators can be used to build more intricate filters. You may compose two phrases and split each one using the or operator to compare two suburbs. You may use the and operator to view values that are inside a range while working with numerical data.

Merge Printing

The phrase "mail merge" refers to the process of merging data in order to create customized publications that can be sent to specific individuals. Directly merging to a printer is an option when creating a merge. The main difference between merge printing and regular printing is that you can choose to print a variety of records.

Put This to the Test:

Equal File

To continue with this experiment, open Mail Merge 6.pub or the preceding file.

- Click Next in the Mail Merge task box. Step 2 of 3: Create consolidated publications. The task pane will display the merging choices.
- To access the Print choices in Backstage view, click Print towards the top of the window.
- Pick a printer to print the document.

- To save paper and ink, we can print more than one certificate per page.

- If you want to print the publication, click [Print]; if not, click the Back arrow to go back to the publication.

- Click on Multiple copies per sheet under options, then choose Multiple pages per sheet. Due to the filter, only the certificates for the three residents of New South Wales will print.

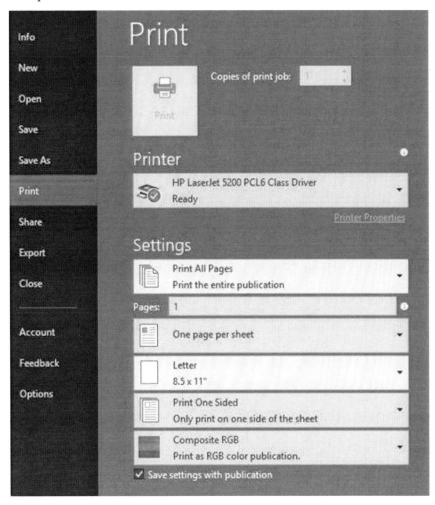

For Your Reference

To merge to a printer:

1. Click on Next: Create merged publications in the Mail Merge task pane

2. Click on Print

3. Select the printer and printing options

4. Click on [Print]

• The Print options enable you to control many print settings, including which merge records to print.

Clicking on Printer Properties allows you to change your printer's properties, as well.

Clearing A Filter

Filters will remain in effect until they are cleared. This applies to any merge results that are printed as well. It is a good idea to reset the filters when you no longer want to work with the filtered data source. This way there will be no chance of inadvertently leaving recipients out. Clearing a filter is accomplished through the Filter and Sort dialog box.

Try This Yourself:

Same File

Open Mail Merge 7.pub or continue using the previous file for this experiment.

- Click Previous in the Mail Merge task window. If required, prepare your publication in Step 3 of the 3 to display Step 2 of 3.
- Click on Edit recipient list to open the Mail Merge Recipients dialog box.
- Click on Filter under Refine recipient list to open the Filter Records tab of the Filter and Sort dialog box.
- Click on [Clear All] to remove all entries.
- Click on [OK], then click [OK] again to go back to the publication. As indicated by the record counter in the Mail Merge task window, all seven records are now present.

For Your Reference

To clear a merge filter:

1. Click on Edit recipient list in the Mail Merge task pane

2. Click on Filter under Refine recipient list

3. Click on [Clear All]

4. Click on [OK], then click on [OK] again

• As well as using the options in the Mail Merge task pane, you can move between records by using the tools in the Preview Results group on the Mailings tab.

Chapter 13

Catalogue Merge!

In This Chapter

- Understanding of the merge area
- Creating a product list
- Selecting a merge area layout
- Inserting text fields
- Formatting text fields
- Inserting picture fields
- Making changes to a catalogue merge
- Merging to a new publication.

INFOCUS

Instead of entering the information for each product or service separately if you need to publish a catalogue of goods or services, you could find it simpler to make a catalogue merge. A catalogue merge takes a list of data from a database and combines it with a publication, much like a mail merge does. The end result will be a catalog with a polished, uniform design as well as a database of product listings that you can access whenever you need to.

Understanding The Merge Area

A catalog merge is similar to a mail merge in that you create or locate a data set, then integrate this information with a publication. Unlike a mail merge, a catalogue merge has a merge area where you may enter the merging fields. Everything you enter in the merge section is repeated throughout the rest of the catalogue.

Displaying The Merge Area

The merge area appears when you pick Catalogue Pages from the Pages group on the Insert tab to begin a catalog merging. On page 2 of the Pages navigation bar, catalog pages appear as three pages that are stacked on top of one another. The number of products on each page of the published catalog and the number of items in the product list used for catalog merging determine how many catalog pages there will be.

The merging area is by default located in the upper left corner of the first catalogue page. It has a border with diagonal lines on it. The size and location of the merging area determine how many items will appear on each catalogue page; for example, the default configuration shows six items per page. It is possible to adjust and change the merging area as necessary, or you may choose a ready-made page layout from the gallery on the Catalogue Tools: fashion tab.

Working With The Merge Area

Each product item in your catalog's merging section may be designed and presented anyway you choose. Publisher will automatically duplicate every item in your product list and pack as many product listings as it can onto each page. Six of the items from the aforementioned example, for instance, would be displayed on each page in three rows of two, with the first item in the list indicating the location of the merging region. Each text field and image field you add in the merging section will display the information for each product in the same spot in each product entry.

By entering the information only once rather than for each product separately, you may save time and work. This is especially useful when creating product catalogues with a lot of goods because it would take a long time to manually enter them all. You can make changes to a single product entry after the catalogue merger is finished, if necessary.

Creating A Product List

The first step in creating a catalog merging is to create a list of the items you wish to include in it. This list of products that are available includes the cost and product ID for each item. If the picture is saved in the same folder as the one where the product list will be saved, you must provide its file name; if not, you must type its full file path.

Put This to the Test:

File Opening

- Before starting this experiment, you MUST OPEN the file Merged Catalogue 1.pub.
- On the Insert tab, choose Catalogue Pages from the Pages group 5.
- ID: 089092
- Price: $109.95
- the pic of messyjessie.jpg
- A new page will load that has a Catalogue Merge Area.
- Click Type a New List on the Catalogue Tools: Format tab, then click Add List in the Start group to display the New Product List dialog box.
- To move the insertion point to the next column, enter Messy Jessie in the Product box and press.
- In the area labeled "Description," type "Children, Humor." An animal by the name of Jessie destroys her small community.
- Complete step 4 again and input the item's ID, cost, and picture as displayed.
- Click [New Entry] to start a new record.
- To create the displayed product list, repeat steps 5 and 6. Then click [OK].
- After opening the course files folder, type "Product list" in the File name field.
- Choose [Save], then [OK].

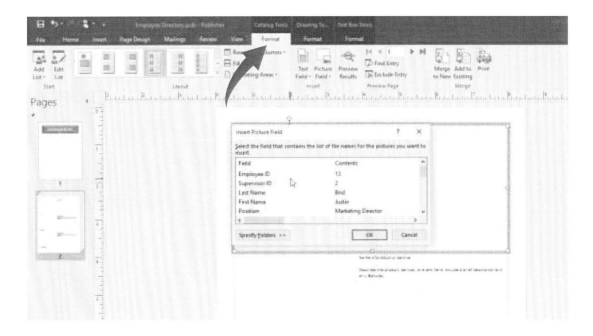

Just for Information

Make a product list by:

1. Select Catalogue Pages from the Pages group by clicking the Insert tab.

2. Select Type a New List under Add List in the Start group on the Catalogue Tools: Format tab.

3. Type the details, then click on [OK]

4. Navigate to the desired save location, type a file name, click on [Save], then click on [OK].

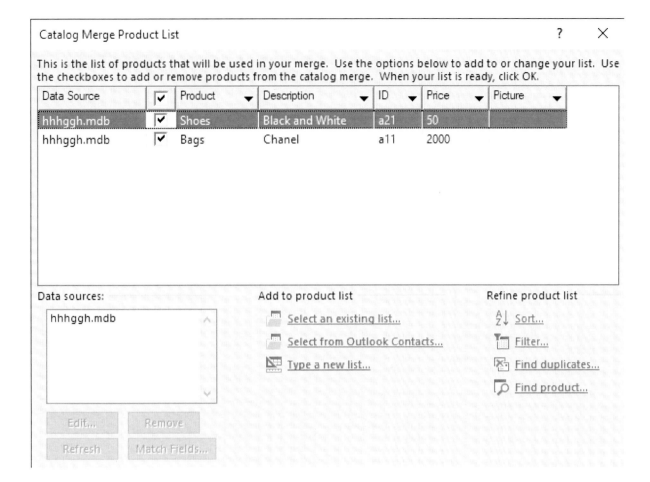

Insert merge fields

You should now organize the information you want to display in your publication. To layout the page, merge fields are added to the catalog merge area. Each merging field in the catalog merge area corresponds to a column in your data source and displays how the information in one record will be displayed.

You may arrange the catalog merging section as you like, and you can specify how many times it repeats on each page after that. For instance, you could want to show four things on each page.

Every item will show up consistently, depending on how the catalog merging area is configured. It is possible to alter the size of each item as well as the size of the catalog merging area.

Important

When you finish your merging, merge fields that you added outside the catalog merge area won't reoccur.

- The merge area layout option
- Choose one of the following actions in the Layout group:
- Choose from one of the galleries of ready-made designs Options for catalog merging layout
- From the Rows and Columns drop-down menu, choose how many rows and columns each page will have.
- Rows and columns used in catalog page layout

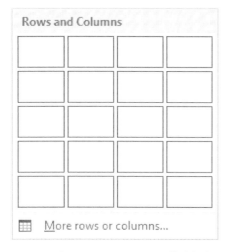

- Insert text merge fields into the catalog merge area
- Click the Text Field button, and click the first merge field that you want to insert.

Product

Description

ID

Price

Picture

Text fields can be added to a catalog merging.

- Select the merge field in the catalog merge area, and then use the following commands to move and resize the merge field:

- Position the mouse pointer over the merging field and hold it there until the Move pointer appears.

- Pointer movement is followed by dragging the merging field to a new location.

- Place the mouse pointer on one of the text box or image frame's sizing handles and hold it there until the pointer changes to the Resize pointer to resize the merging field. Drag the mouse to adjust the text box or picture frame's size after moving the ruler's points.

- In order to deselect the merging field, click outside of it.

- Once you've added all the fields you require from your data source, repeat Steps 1-3.

Important

- The fields are added at the current point of insertion (insertion point blinking cursor). The merging field will be added to a new textbox and inserted there if there isn't an insertion point.

- Set the text merge fields' formatting

- By styling the merging fields in your catalog merge template, you may format the combined catalog data. You can enter merged items as well as non-merged text and formatting in these fields just like any other text box.

- Select the field holding the data you wish to format in the catalog merge template, together with the merge field characters that surround it («« »»).
- Choose the options you desire from the Text Box Tools menu.
- Fill in the catalog merge section with photo merge fields.
- Select the first merging field you wish to enter by clicking the Picture Field button.
- Select the merge field in the catalog merge area, and then use the following commands to move and resize the merge field:
- Position the mouse pointer over the merging field and hold it there until the Move pointer appears. The merging field may be moved by moving the cursor and then dragging it.
- Place the mouse pointer on one of the handles on the text box or image frame and hold it there until the pointer changes to the Resize pointer to resize the merging field. Drag the mouse to resize the cursor, then size the text box or picture frame to your preference.
- In order to deselect the merging field, click outside of it.
- Once you've added all the fields you require from your data source, repeat Steps 1-3.

Important:

The fields are added at the current point of insertion (insertion point blinking cursor). If there isn't an insertion point, a new textbox will be made, and this new textbox will include the merging field.

Move or resize the catalog merge area

You can enlarge the catalog merge area if your prepared merge fields no longer fit within it. You might need to fit fewer items or records on each page if you raise the size. To pick the Catalog Merge Area, click on it.

Drag the mouse after positioning it on one of the handles on the Catalog Merge Area.

Enter the numbers you want for items across the page and down the page on the Catalog

Merge Layout toolbar to specify how many things should display on each page.

Finish and preview the template

• Click Preview Results.

• Click the arrows to view each page of merged data.

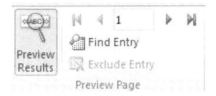

Collection of catalog previews

• Click the item you want to exclude from the list after selecting Exclude Entry from the Preview Page group.

Top Page

• Complete your catalog publication, print it, and save it.

• You have three choices to accomplish the merge:

• Your combined publication is immediately printable.

• A new publication with the combined material can be made and printed. Just as you may with any other publication in Publisher, you can edit the content of this one.

• As there can only be one set of catalog pages per publication, if you wish to include numerous catalog merges in the publication, you will need to make a new one.

• You can add the merged content to an existing publication.

• Create a new publication or add your material to an existing publication if you wish to add a front and rear cover or any additional pages to your magazine.

Combining into a new publication

• You may gather and save all of your merged pages as a single new combined publication that has the real data — for example, product names and prices — instead of merge fields if you wish to amend your merged pages, store them for later use, or print them at a later time.

- Click Merge to New under the Merge group.

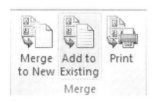

You can save and edit the new publication that Publisher produces. Even front and back cover pages are an option. Make sure the total number of pages in your catalog is a multiple of four if you intend to print it as a booklet.

To do this:

- Click Save this publication in the Catalog Merge task box.
- Give your new publication a name in the File name box, then click Save.

- Save any adjustments you made to your catalog merge template as well, if required. When you change

- The data in your data source, you may utilize this catalog merge template once again to produce more merged pages.

Adding to an existing publication

You can upload your integrated material directly if your covers are already set up in a different publication or if you want the catalog to appear at the conclusion of a longer publication.

Make sure your catalog merge template matches the existing publication in the following ways before adding your merged pages at the end of it:

- Page width (height and width)

- View of page (one-page spread or two-page spread)

- Type of publication (Web or print)

- A page order (left-to-right or right-to-left)

- A publication that is already open cannot have merged pages added. Make careful to save and shut the publication you wish to combine with if you are currently working on it before you finish your merging.

- Click Add to Existing in the Merge group.

Merging a catalog with an existing publication

- Locate and choose the publication you wish to add the combined pages to in the Open Publication dialog box, and then click Open.

- Publisher concludes the current publishing by including the combined pages.

- Tip Click any page you wish to relocate in the page navigation pane, then drag it to the desired spot

- In your new publication to rearrange the pages.

- To save your adjustments to an existing publication, click Save.

- Save any adjustments you made to your catalog merge template as well, if required.

- When you change the data in your data source, you may utilize this catalog merge template once again to produce more merged pages.

- Print the combined document.

- Choose Print from the Merge group.

- Combine catalog to print

- The BackStage view of the print page is displayed by Publisher.

Selecting A Merge Area Layout

The catalog layout choices appear in the Layout group on the Catalogue Tools: Format tab once you've generated or selected a product list to utilize in your catalog. You may use these settings to decide how many goods will be shown on each page and how the product details will be presented.

Put This to the Test:

Equal File

Open the Merged Catalogue 2.pub file to continue with this experiment using the previous file.

• Ensure the Catalogue Tools: Format tab is active, then click on the first option in the merge area layout gallery in the Layout group. This option will display one product on each page.

• Click on the second layout option in the gallery. This option will display two products on each page.

• Click on the More arrow for the layout gallery, then select the option 4 entries, 2 columns. This option will display four products on each page – two at the top and two at the bottom.

• On the Catalogue Tools: Format tab, click on Fill Order in the Layout group, then ensure Across then down is selected

By doing this, you can make sure that the second item in the list will appear above the first one rather than below it.

For Your Information

To alter the arrangement of the merging area:

1. Select the Format tab under Catalogue Tools.

2. Pick a layout from the gallery in the Layout group.

3. You may select the number of product rows and columns to display on each page of your catalogue. Simply pick the number of rows and columns from the grid by clicking on the Catalogue Tools: Format tab, then clicking on Rows and Columns in the Layout group.

4. Make sure the Catalogue Tools: Format tab is chosen, then click on Text Field in the Insert group, then pick Product. The first item in the product list that is visible in the text field is called Messy Jessie.

5.　　To edit the text, click inside the text box. Add the price, order number, and other details to this text box, then repeat step 2

6.　　On the Catalogue Tools: Format tab, select Price from the Text Field drop-down menu in the Insert group.

7.　　Press and then repeat step 6 to select ID.

8.　　Click outside the merging area to see the changes to the rest of the page.

9.　　Click outside the merging area to see the changes to the rest of the page. It's a bit difficult to view the other four products on the page, but you can see that their information was instantly inserted.

Inserting Text Fields

In order to add text fields:

1. To insert the text field, click on the merge area.

2. Select the Text Field option under the Insert group on the Catalogue Tools: Format tab.

3. Choose the required text area.

• The text field will appear in a new text box within the merging area if you don't click within an existing text box before inserting a text field.

Formatting Text Fields

Formatting text in merge fields is the same as formatting text in regular text boxes. The sole distinction is that formatting text in a merging field instantly formats the relevant text fields in the rest of the catalogue. By doing this, you may avoid inconsistent catalog design and avoid spending time individually formatting each product item.

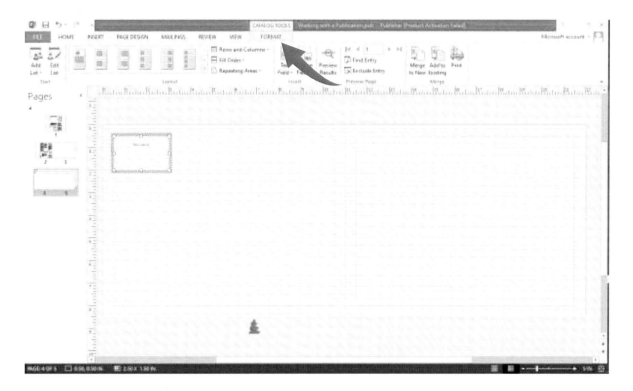

Try It Yourself with the Same File

- Click the Home tab, select 20 from the drop-down menu for Font Size under the Font group, and the product name will now be this size.

- Select the text Messy Jessie by clicking on the text box that holds the product name and description in the merging area.

- Repeat steps 2 to change the product description to size 12 after selecting the remaining text in the text box. To make the text bold, select Bold from the Font group on the Home tab.

- To make the font size 12 and Bold for the product price, repeat steps 2 and 3.

- To see the changes to the rest of the page, click outside of the merging area. Repeat step 2 after selecting the product ID to change the text's size to 10.

For Your Information

Formatting text fields

1. Pick the text box that needs styling.

2. Make the required alterations.

• Any formatting you can apply to normal text may be used in text fields in a catalogue merging. This indicates that you must take care to make sure that the formatting you apply to text fields is appropriate and understandable, just as when working with plain text.

Inserting Picture Fields

Most catalogs have photos of the advertised items. You can refine your content to improve the design of your book or to better convey information about your product. Before adding an image field, make sure the photo you want to use is the same size and location. Images of different sizes are not displayed correctly.

Put This to the Test:

- Click the Merge area and then click the photo icon in the center of the image placeholder to open the Insert Photo Field dialog box. Make sure the Image category is selected as shown.

- Click [OK] to enter the information in the photo box. Because the image is larger than the placeholder, only part of each image is visible.

- To resize the image as shown, repeat step 4 and drag the bottom middle and right handles to the right. Move the upper medium size handle of the image with the mouse until a double-headed arrow appears.

- Click and drag the image to the right to center it in the column. Then click outside the merging area to increase the visibility of the photo..

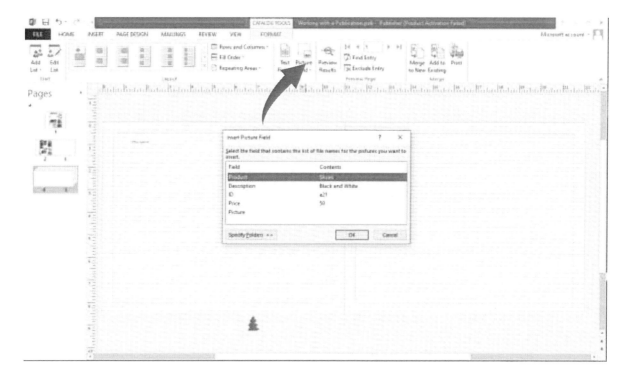

For Your Reference

To insert a picture field:

1. Select the icon in the center of the empty image placeholder.

2. Select the "Photos" category and click [OK].

3. Resize the image if necessary.

• An unlimited number of photo fields can be added. On the Catalog Tools tab, in the Insert group, click Image Field and select the appropriate category.

Previewing And Modifying A Catalogue Merge

As with any creative process, it's a good idea to review and check each product listing for errors or layout issues before finalizing the catalog. Although individual product listings can be adjusted after the merge is complete, we recommend changing the layout ahead of time to ensure publishing consistency.

Put This to the Test:

- Catalog Tools: Select the Format tab and click the right arrow in the Template Pages group to go to the second catalog page. The product description at the top left has also been partially deleted.

- Catalog Tools: On the Format tab, in the Model Pages group, click the left arrow to return to the first page of the catalog. Then click on the integration area to activate it.

- To resize the Product Price and ID text boxes, click the box and then move the sizing handle to the bottom center as shown.

- To move the text box down, click and drag the border until four arrows appear at the position of the mouse pointer.

- Click on the product description text box as shown to enlarge. Then repeat steps 4 and 5. The text field can now contain product descriptions.

For Your Information

To see a catalog merging in preview:

1. Select the "Catalogue Tools" link. style tab

2. To navigate through the catalogue pages, click on the arrows in the Preview Page group.

Merging To A New Publication

It's time to convert the merge into a catalogue publication once you've done making modifications to the merging area of your catalogue merge. You can choose to merge with either an existing magazine or a new one. When the merging is finished, the catalogue turns into a regular publication that lets you make specific adjustments without affecting every single item.

Put This to the Test:

- In the Directory Tools window, select the Format tab. Then, in the Merge group, click the Merge New option. The default publication directory and the new publication will open in the merge directories window on the right.

- Click Page 2 in the Pages navigation bar to view the second page of your publication.

- Click on the text box with the phrase "Messy Jesse". This text box no longer has a merge area.

- Click page 3 in the page navigation bar to view the third page of your publication.

- Click in the Kitchen Utensils text box.

- A text box is now active indicating that certain elements of the product can be changed.

For Your Information

Merging with a brand-new publication

1. In the Catalog tool, select the Format tab.

2. In the Merge group, choose Merge New.

• Catalog Tools: Select the Format tab, in the Merge group, click Add to Existing, scroll to Publications, and choose whether you want to add catalog pages to an existing publication. The combined page is added to the publication summary..

Chapter 14

Saving and Sharing

In This Chapter

- Sending a publication as an email
- Changing the file type of a publication
- Saving a publication as a JPEG
- Learning how to save a publication for a commercial printer
- Learning how to save a publication for another computer.

INFOCUS

After you create a post, the next step in the process is to publish it so others can share it. If you have access to a printer, you can print from home, but there are several other options that can help simplify the sharing process and produce more professional publications..

Create a newsletter

- Click Include > Newsletters and scroll down to find the Newsletter category.
- (In Publisher 2021, click the most popular newsletters.)
- Select a template and under Customize, click the color scheme and font scheme you want.
- Click on the required business information set or create a new one.
- From Options, select Single Page Spread (if you want to print one or both sides of the newsletter) or Double Page Spread (if you are working with a front page design and want to print the newsletter tabloid as a printable). paper).).

338

- To send the customer's address in a newsletter rather than a separate envelope, select the Include Customer's Address check box.

- Click Create.

- Modify the template to include items you will reuse in future newsletters, such as titles and logos.

- Save your new template and, from the Save As dialog that appears, navigate to the location and folder you want, choose Publisher Template in the Save as type box.

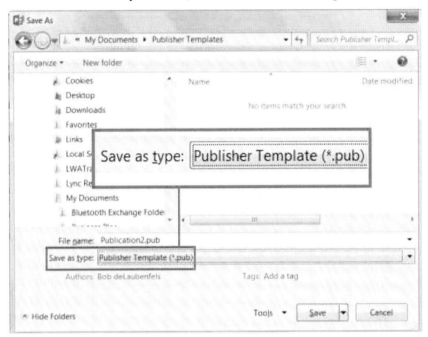

Tip: You can tell the editor where to save the template. Go to File > Options > Save and enter the path to the folder where you want to add all the templates instead of the default location of the individual template. This will also enable a new tab called Customize when you create a new post, which will contain all of your custom templates.

If you want to change your newsletter, you can add pages or remove pages from the newsletter. You can also print your newsletter on paper or 11x17 paper and create and send a newsletter via email to avoid shipping costs entirely.

Make design changes to the layout

- On the Page Design tab, click Options and click the desired number of columns for each page.

- On internal pages (eg pages 2 and 3 of a 4-page newsletter), the option to select the page to change appears. Click the left button on the subpage or the right button on the subpage, and then click one of the following formats for each page: 3 stories, calendar, order form, reply form, or support form.

Work with the text

If you have already created a company information kit, your contact information and logo will automatically replace a placeholder text.

Note: Company records do not automatically replace placeholder text in templates downloaded from Office Online. To replace the placeholder names, addresses, and logos with your business information, click the smart tag button ⓘ for a business information item, such as the company name or address, and then click Update from Business Information Set. (The smart tag button appears when you point to text or a logo.)

For each block of placeholder text, do one of the following:

- Select and enter the placeholder text.

- To select the placeholder text, right-click, select Change Text from the context menu, select Text File, click the file that contains the text you want to use, and then click OK.

Note: In most cases, the text will automatically fit into the text box. For example, long article titles will automatically shrink to fit the text. Resize the text. DO one of the following:

To prevent text from automatically resizing to fit a text box that is not bound to another text box, click the text box, and on the Text Box Tools Format tab, click Fit Text > Auto Fit. Select the text that you want to change, and then on the Text Box Formatting Tools tab, in the Font Size list, click a different font size.

For more information about using text boxes, see Fit text in text boxes..

340

Utilize the images

Right-click the placeholder image, point to Change Image, click Change Image, and then click Insert to select a new image from one of the available sources in the Insert Image dialog box.

Tip: If you don't see the Change Image command when you right-click, click the image placeholder once until a white ring appears around the image frame. One of the images is surrounded by a gray circle with an x, click on it again and choose "Right Click" from the menu..

Sending A Publication As An Email

If your publication is for one person or people at a distance, it may not be the most effective way to spread the word. In this case, you can choose to send the publication by email. Publisher gives you a number of options for doing this, including adding your work to other file types.

Put This to the Test:

File Opening

Before starting this experiment, it is important to open the Save and Share 1.pub file.

- Select the Files tab, then select Sharing Options. Available lines can be emailed to publications.

- In the right pane, select Submit Current Page. Email options are displayed above the displayed post.

- When prompted, enter recipient@emailaddress.com in the To field.

- After clicking Greetings, you must enter a subject area.

- At this point, we usually click Send, but we don't want to send it.

- Click [Cancel] to stop receiving emails.

For Your Information

Sending an email with a publication:

1. Click on the File tab, then click on Share

2. Click on the desired option in the right pane

3. Type the required email details

4. Click on [Send]

• The three other choices open your emailing application and send the publication as a Publisher, PDF, or XPS attachment that must be downloaded and viewed by the recipient, as opposed to the [Send Current Page] option, which delivers the publication as the body of the email.

Changing The File Type

There may be some compatibility issues when distributing magazines electronically. For example, the person you're sharing your publication with may not have Publisher installed at all or may have an outdated version. Fortunately, you can change the file format of your publication to make it compatible with other programs.

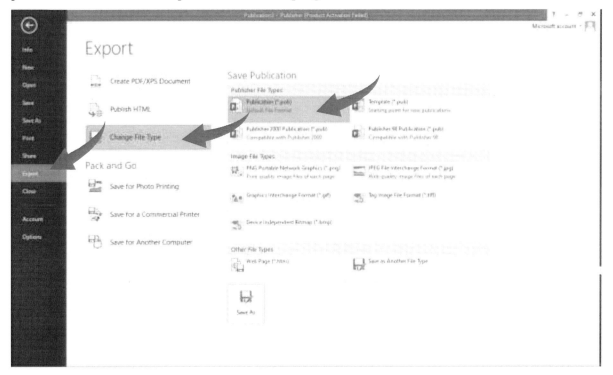

Put This to the Test:

Equal File

- To continue practicing with previous files, open Save and Share 2.pub.

- Select the File tab and click the Export button. In the middle panel, choose Change File Type. The available file types are listed.

- In Publisher file type, select Publisher 2021 Publications (*.pub).

- If you select [Save As], the Save As dialog box appears. The file name must be File Publisher 2021. Navigate to the Course Files folder and click Save. This message warns readers that some elements of the publication will not work correctly with the new file format.

- Choose Yes to save as a Publisher 2021 file for notes.

To change the file format of a publication:

1. Select the Export option from the File tab.

2. Select Modify File Type.

3. After choosing a file format, click [Save As].

4. Type a file name, select a place to store it, and then click [Save].

A publication's file type can be changed right from the Save As dialog box. Simply pick a file type by clicking on the drop-down arrow next to Save as type.

Saving For Photo Printing

Publisher provides you the option of storing your publication in the JPEG or TIFF format, which you may use to print from a photo printer or make a picture book. The publication's name will be added to a folder that is created if you choose this option, and each page will be saved there as a separate JPEG or TIFF file.

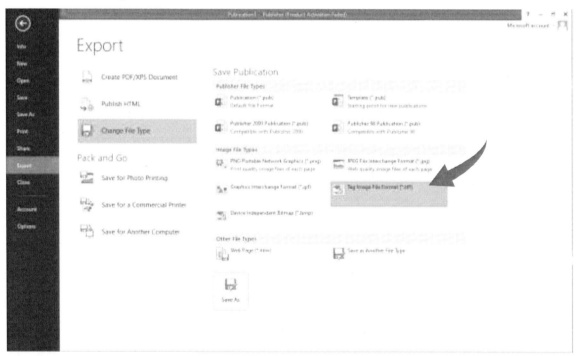

Put This to the Test:

- Click the File tab under Pack and Go and then click Save to print the photo.

- In the right pane, click the drop-down arrow next to Save photos for printing to see the options. You can choose to save your photos in JPEG or TIFF format.

- Click Save Image Set to open the Choose Location dialog box and select the JPEG image from which you want to print the photos.

- To save the publication, make sure the Course Files folder is visible, then Choose Folder. Check out the new JPEG now.

- After launching Explorer, navigate to the Course Files folder. You now have a new folder in your Course Files folder that is identical to your publication.

- Double-click to display a folder. Each publication page is saved as a separate JPEG file.

For Your Information

When saving a document as a JPEG or TIFF:

1. Select the Export option from the File tab.

2. Under Pack and Go, select Save for Photo Printing.

3. Click [Save Image Set] after selecting the preferred format under Save for Photo Printing.

4. After selecting a saving place, click [Select folder].

Saving For A Commercial Printer

Your printing needs may exceed what your printer can do.

Commercial printing services with different printing needs such as quantity, quality, size and binding of books can help you. Before printing your publication, check with your print shop for information such as acceptable file formats and targets.

Put This to the Test:

- Open the Save and Share 4.pub file to continue experimenting with the previous file.

- Go to the File tab, select Export, then under Packaging and Shipping, select Save for Commercial Printers.

- Make sure Publisher, PDF and Commercial Press are all available.

- As you can see, the pub file is selected under Save for Commercial Printers.

- Click the [Package and Copy Wizard] button to open the Package and Copy Wizard dialog box.

- Click another location to select it, then click [Browse] to open the Choose Location dialog box.

- After moving to the Course Files folder, click the [Select Folder] button.

- By clicking [Next], the document is ready for printing.

- Click here. Uncheck it, print a composite proof and click [OK]. Compressed ("extracted") folders containing publications can now be imported into print services.

For Your Reference

To save a publication for a commercial printer:

1. Click on the File tab, then click on Export

2. Click on Save for a Commercial Printer

3. Select the desired options, then click on [Pack and Go Wizard]

4. Choose a save location, click on [Next], then click on [OK]

• Not all commercial printers will accept Publisher files, but most will accept PDF. Selecting the option to pack both a Publisher and a PDF file allows the printing service to choose the best way to print your publication for you.

Saving For Another Computer

If you want to share, you can choose to save your publication with these layouts.

It is not clear what other electronics and fonts, graphics, etc. are compatible with their machines. This allows others to open and edit the document without losing components or encountering compatibility issues.

Try this:

- Open the Save and Share 5.pub file to continue experimenting with the previous file.

- Select the File tab to select export options.

- Select and save to another computer.

- Click the [Package and Delivery Wizard] button to open the Package and Deliver wizard dialog box, and then click the [Next] button.

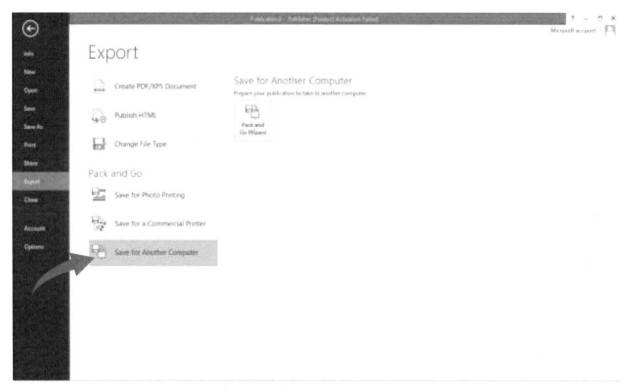

• Click on Other location to select it, then click on [Browse] to display the Choose Location dialog box

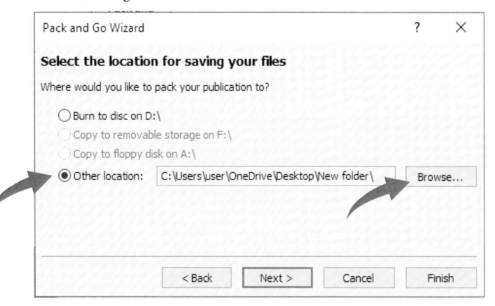

• Navigate to the course files folder, then click on [Select folder]

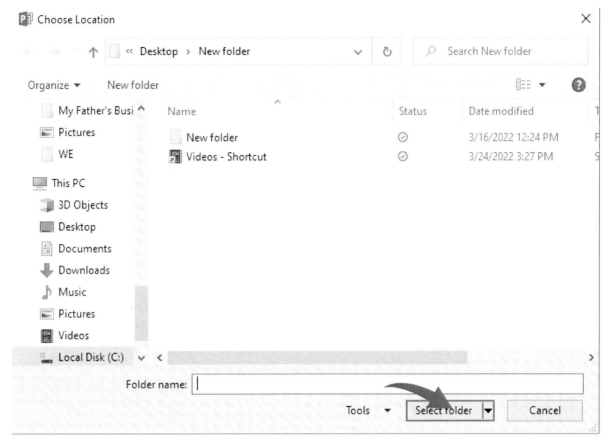

- Click on [Next]

- Click on Embed TrueType fonts and Create links for embedded graphics so that all three options are ticked, as shown

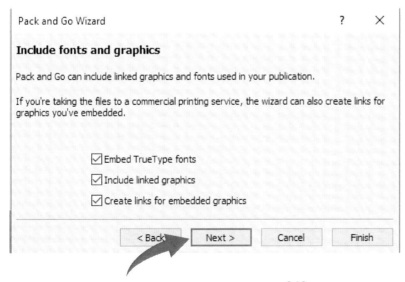

• Click on [Next], click on [Finish], then click on [OK]. The publication is now saved in a compressed ("zipped") folder which can be opened on another computer.

For Your Reference

To save a publication for another computer:

1. Click on the File tab, then click on Export

2. Click on Save for Another Computer

3. Click on [Pack and Go Wizard]

4. Choose a save location, then click on [Next]

5. Select the desired options, click on [Next], then click on [Finish].

Chapter 15

Getting Help and Keyboard Shortcuts

In This Chapter

- Understanding how Publisher Help works

- Accessing the Help window

- Navigating the Help window

- Using Google to find help.

- Learning all the keyboard shortcuts

INFOCUS

Microsoft Publisher's interface is intuitive and easy to use, but there are always things you don't fully understand or need help with. This is where help comes in handy.

Understanding How Help Works

You can use the Help features and tools in Office. The Editor Help window is the main entry point to Help. This window opens when you indicate specific instructions in a specific dialog box or click on the ribbon.

Tip: Help systems are usually dynamic because Microsoft's web content is very easy to edit or update. As a result, the Help window for Publisher may look slightly different.

Help tools

These tools are designed to make working in the editor help window easier. It includes back and forward buttons and a print button that you can use to review topics you've studied. You can quickly return to the main editor help screen by pressing the Home button.

Search box: You can use the search box to display the information you are looking for. Enter the name of the topic or term for which you need help or information.

Top Categories

This is a list of frequently searched topics that may be related to the topic you are looking for information about. Click the plus icon next to one of them to display all help articles related to that general feature or topic. While working on the sticky icon worksheet, you can keep the editor help window open by clicking the sticky icon labeled Keep help on top/Don't keep help on top.

If you select Keep help at the top, the button icon will change to Don't keep help, so you can easily turn this feature off again.

Accessing The Help Window

The Publisher Help window is available in three main places in Publisher. You can access general help by clicking Help for Publisher in the Publisher window. Help for a specific dialog box can be opened by clicking the Help button in the dialog box, and command-specific help can be opened by pointing to the command and clicking the command.

Try This Yourself:

Open File

Before starting this exercise ensure that you have a blank publication open.

- Click Microsoft Publisher Help on the right side of the title bar. The Publisher Help window opens and displays the main Publisher Help screen.

- Click Close to close the Publisher Help window.

- Click the Page Design tab, and then click the dialog box launcher for the Page Setup group to display the Page Setup dialog box.

- Click the Help button in the upper right corner of the dialog box. An editor help window appears with suggestions for page size and page setup.

- Click Close to close the Editor Help dialog box and click Cancel to close the Page Setup dialog box. You can also access Publisher Help for specific commands.

- Click the Insert tab, point to Picture in the Pictures group, and click . This is very useful when inserting images.

- Click Close to close the Publisher Help window.

Support

? Microsoft Office Help

Getting Started

Contact Us

Tools for Working With Office

Options

Product Activated

Microsoft Office Professional Plus 2010

This product contains Microsoft Access, Microsoft SharePoint Workspace, Microsoft OneNote, Micros Microsoft PowerPoint, Microsoft Publisher, Micros InfoPath.

Change Product Key

About Microsoft Publisher

For Your Reference

To access Help:

- Click on Microsoft Publisher Help, or

- Open a dialog box and click on Help, or

- Point to a command and press, or

- Press

- Specific Help isn't available for every command; however, if you point to a command, a tooltip will appear including a description of the tool and below this (if specific help is available) the text Tell me more. Clicking on Tell me more will display the Help topics for that command.

Navigating the Help Window

The Microsoft Publisher Help window includes a series of buttons that you can use to navigate between Help topics, such as the Forward and Back arrows, which allow you to move back and forth between the pages you visit. There is also the Home button which allows you to return to the Home screen without having to scroll through previous pages.

Try This Yourself:

Before starting this exercise ensure you have a publication open.

- Click on the Microsoft Publisher Help tool to display the Publisher Help window
- Under Top categories, click on Work with pictures and watermarks to display a list of articles
- Click on Crop a picture to open the article
- Click on Back to return to the list of categories
- Click in the search box and type font, then press to display articles related to fonts
- Click on Remove languages and fonts you don't use to display the article
- Click on Home to return to the home screen
- Click on Close to exit the Publisher Help window

For Your Reference

To navigate forward or backward:

- Click on the Forward or Back arrow. To go to the Home screen:
- Click on Home

• You can increase the size of the text in the Publisher Help window by clicking on Use Large Text, located immediately to the left of the search box. Simply click on Use Large Text again if you wish to return to the default font size.

Using Google to Get Help

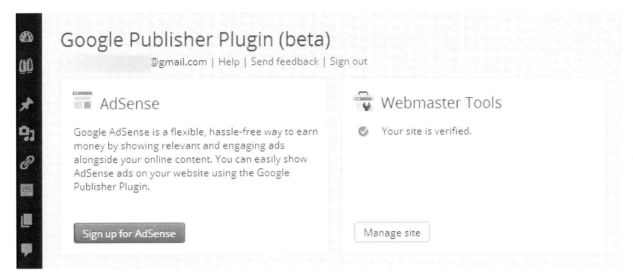

If you're having problems with Microsoft Office or would like to find some quicker and easier ways of working with Office, you can rest assured that others have had similar concerns and have posted tips and possible solutions on the web.

Using a popular search engine such as Google can easily put you in touch with a range of information from other users.

Try This Yourself:

Before starting this exercise ensure you have a publication open.

• Open your web browser in the normal way and access the Google website (www.google.com.au)

• Type Microsoft Publisher 2021 into the search box and press

• After a few moments a range of suggested sites will appear. Since the web is dynamic and constantly changing, your results will most likely differ.

• Scroll through and follow any links you find interesting

- Close the browser window

For Your Reference

To Google help for Publisher:

1. Open your web browser in the normal way and access the Google website

2. Type the desired search criteria in the search box and click on [Google Search]

• This type of help tends to be more eclectic than direct help from Microsoft Office. Instead of an organized help system, by using a Google search you'll find plenty of help and support, but also opinions (both good and bad), commentary, observations, and a whole range of other information.

Concluding Remarks

Congratulations!

You have now completed Getting Started with Microsoft Publisher. Getting Started with Microsoft Publisher was designed to get you to the point where you can competently perform a variety of operations. We have tried to build up your skills and knowledge by having you work through specific tasks.

The step-by-step approach will serve as a reference for you when you need to repeat a task.

Where To From Here?

The following is a little advice about what to do next:

- Play around with what you've learned for a while. Use some of the application's instructions to practice the abilities you have already learned. This will determine how much of the ideas and characteristics have persisted.

- Some components of the course may at this time be a little hazy, so avoid doing a huge assignment just now if you can. Review some of the areas where you might need further clarification. These step-by-step notes were created to assist you in the classroom and at work. Use the examples and exercises in them, then try again.

Here are some tips and tricks we've discovered to be useful for learning more about technology:

- If you have the knowledge and resources, read computer periodicals since they frequently contain helpful information about certain approaches

- If your software has a manual, which is uncommon these days, spend some time each day reading a few pages.

- If your software came with a manual (which is rare these days), take an interest in what your work colleagues have done and how they did it.

- Try the strategies out right away and you'll learn a lot over time. There are also more courses and books available for you to work through. Interested in More?

Keyboard Shortcuts

Shape and Picture Effect Shortcut

(Microsoft, 2022)

Actions	Shortcuts
the Shape Effects Menu is opened	Press: JD, SE, Alt
launching the Shadow Gallery for Shape Effects	To select an option, press Alt, JD, SE, and S.
the Shape Effects - Reflection Gallery is opened	Press Alt, JD, SE, and R. Then, select an option.
The Shape Effects - Glow Gallery is now open.	Press Alt, JD, SE, and G- before selecting an option.
launching the Soft Edges Gallery for Shape Effects	Press Alt, JD, SE, and E. Then, select an option.
the Shape Effects - Bevel Gallery has opened	Press Alt, JD, SE, and B. Then, select an option.
The Shape Effects - 3-D Rotation Gallery is now open.	Press Alt, JD, SE, and D, then select an option.
the Shape Styles Gallery is opened	To navigate the choices, press Alt, JD, and ST.

Picture effects Shortcut

Actions	Shortcuts
the Picture Effects Menu is opened	Press: JP, PE, Alt
opening the Shadow Gallery for Picture Effects	To select an option, press Alt, JP, PE, and S.
launching the Reflection Gallery under Picture Effects	To select an option, press Alt, JP, PE, and R.

the Picture Effects - Glow Gallery is opened	Tap Alt, JP, PE, and G, then select an option.
launching the Soft Edges Gallery for Picture Effects	Press Alt, JP, PE, and E. Then, select an option.
the Picture Effects - Bevel Gallery has opened	Tap Alt, JP, PE, and B, then select an option.
The Picture Effects - 3-D Rotation Gallery is now open.	To select an option, press Alt, JP, PE, and D.
the Picture Styles Gallery is opened	press the keys Alt, JP, and K, then select an option.
Changing the image style	Press Alt, JP, K, and C.

Text Effects Shortcuts

Actions	Shortcuts
Dropdown with Text Fill opened	Press: Alt, JX, and TI
No More Fill Colors Fill	Press Alt, JX, TI, N, then tab through the available options.
Adding Effects	To select an option, press Alt, JX, TI, and M.
Tints	To select an option, press Alt, JX, TI, and F.
Type of Font Color	Press Alt, JX, TI, T, then tab through the available options.
Dropdown with Text Fill opened	Press Alt, JX, TI, and S.

Text outline dropdown shortcut

Actions	Shortcuts
Opening Text Diagram Dropdown	Press Alt, JX, and TO.
Taking Outline Off	Press Alt, JX, TO, and N.

Further Outline Colors	Press Alt, JX, TO, and M, then select an option.
Outline Effects...	To select an option, press Alt. JX.TO.O.
Sample Line Color	To select an option, press Alt, JX, TO, and S.
Weight	To select an option, press Alt, JX, TO, and W.
Dashes	Press Alt, JX, TO, D, then tab through the available options.

Text effects dropdown shortcut

Actions	Shortcuts
Opening Text Effects Dropdown	Press: JX, TE, Alt
Shadow	To select an option, press Alt, JX, TE, and S.
Reflection	To select an option, press Alt, JX, TE, and R.
Glow	To select an option, press Alt, JX, TE, and G.
Bevel	To select an option, press Alt, JX, TE, and B.

Create, Opening, Closing, or save a publication shortcuts

Actions	Shortcuts
Opening a new instance of Publisher	Press: CTRL+N
Displaying the Opening Publication dialog box	Press: CTRL+O
Closing the current publication	Press: CTRL+F4 or CTRL+W
Displaying the Save As dialog box	Press: CTRL+S

Edit or format text or objects shortcuts

Actions	Shortcuts

the Find option selected, the Find and Replace task window appearing	Press F3, CTRL+F, or SHIFT+F4 to start.
displaying the Replace option selected in the Find and Replace task pane	Press CTRL+H
spelling check	Press CTRL+H
the task window for the thesaurus is shown	the keys SHIFT+F7
the Research task pane being shown	ALT + click a word to activate
choosing all of the text (If the cursor is in a text box, this Selects all text in the current story; if the cursor is not in a text box, this Selects all the objects on a page.)	Input: CTRL+A
Adding bold to text	Input: CTRL+B
text in italics	Input: CTRL+I
highlighting text	Input: CTRL+U
Making text smaller or switching from upper to lower case in small capital letters	Then, press: CTRL+SHIFT+K
the Font dialog is displayed	CTRL+SHIFT+F is pressed
Copying the format	CTRL+SHIFT+C is pressed
formatting paste	Then Press: CTRL+SHIFT+V
Activate or deactivate special characters	CTRL+SHIFT+Y is pressed
Character formatting should be restored to the current text style.	CTRL+SPACEBAR is pressed
Subscript formatting can be used or removed.	The CTRL+= key

the use of superscript formatting or its removal	CTRL+SHIFT+=, press
increasing the distance between words' letters (kerning)	[CTRL+SHIFT+]
reduce the distance between words' letters (kerning)	Click: CTRL+SHIFT+[
an increase of 1.0 point in font size	Click: CTRL+]
Font size should be shrunk by 1 point.	Click: CTRL+[
Increasing the font size to the following setting	CTRL+SHIFT+> is pressed
Reduce the font size to the following size.	CTRL+SHIFT+< is pressed
Aligning a paragraph in four different ways: in the center, on the left, on the right, and on both sides (justified)	Input: CTRL+E
Place each paragraph in an even horizontal line.	Input: CTRL+L
Put a paragraph's newspaper alignment in place (East Asian languages only)	Input: CTRL+R
the dialog window for hyphenation	Input: CTRL+J
adding the present time	CTRL+SHIFT+D is pressed
adding the present day's date	Then, press CTRL+SHIFT+J
the current page number being inserted	CTRL+SHIFT+H is pressed
If a word appears at the end of a line, avoid hyphenating it.	Then, press ALT+SHIFT+T
the use of superscript formatting or its removal	Hit ALT+SHIFT+D
increasing the distance between words' letters (kerning)	Then, press ALT+SHIFT+P
reduce the distance between words' letters (kerning)	CTRL+SHIFT+0 is pressed (zero)

Copying text formats shortcuts

Actions	Shortcuts
Copying formatting from the Selected text	Ctrl+Shift+C is pressed.
Applying copied formatting to text	Then, press CTRL+SHIFT+V.

Copying, cut, Pasting or delete text or objects shortcuts

Actions	Shortcuts
The Selected Text or Object Being Copied	Click or tap CTRL+C or CTRL+INSERTING.
Text or object selected for cutting	SHIFT+DELETE or CTRL+X to delete.
Text or an object can be pasted	Alternatively, use SHIFT+INSERT.
Delete the chosen item	Simply click DELETE or CTRL+SHIFT+X.

Undo or redo an action shortcuts

Actions	Shortcuts
Undo the last thing you did.	Press the ALT+BACKSPACE or CTRL+Z keys.
Replicate what you just did.	Click CTRL+Y or F4.

Layer objects shortcuts

Actions	Shortcuts
Bring the item up front	Input: ALT+F6
send the item back	Press ALT + SHIFT + F6.

Snap objects shortcuts

Actions	Shortcuts
Press F10, SHIFT+R, SHIFT+S, or SHIFT+M to turn on or off Snap to Guides.	

Selecting or group objects shortcuts

Actions	Shortcuts
selecting all of the page's objects (If your cursor is in a text box, this Selects all the text in a story)	Input: CTRL+A
Selected items can be grouped or ungrouped.	Ctrl+Shift+G is pressed.
Remove the Selected Text's Selection	Input: Escape key
From a selected object, remove the selection.	Input: Escape key
selecting the group's object if it has the text "Selected"	Input: Escape key

Work with pages shortcuts

Choosing or Inserting pages

These commands Apply to the specified two-page spread if your publication is in a two-page spread view. Otherwise, they solely Apply to the page that was chosen.

Actions	Shortcuts
activating the Go To Page dialog box	Press F5 or CTRL + G.
Adding a page or two of text here. If you are creating a newsletter, it opens the dialog box for adding publications of the type Pages.	CTRL+SHIFT+N is pressed.
placing a new page after the existing one.	CTRL+SHIFT+U is pressed.

Move between pages shortcuts

Actions	Shortcuts
the Go To Page dialog box being seen.	Press F5 or CTRL + G.
visiting the following page	Then, press CTRL+PAGE DOWN.
navigating to the prior page	Hit CTRL+PAGE UP.
the master page and the current page being switched between	Input: CTRL+M

Use the master page shortcut

Actions	Shortcuts
Switching between the current page and the master page.	Press: CTRL+M

Show or hide boundaries or guides shortcuts

Actions	Shortcuts
On or off Boundaries.	CTRL+SHIFT+O is pressed.
Turn on or off the horizontal baseline guides (not available in web view)	Input: CTRL+F7
Turn on or off the Vertical Baseline Guides (only available in East Asian languages; not in online view).	Then, press CTRL+SHIFT+F7.

Zoom shortcuts

Actions	Shortcuts
Changing the size of the actual object and the current view	Input F9
Click to enlarge the page.	CTRL+SHIFT+L is pressed.

Printing shortcuts

Using Print Preview
These keyboard shortcuts are available when you're in Print view and affect the print preview pane.

Actions	Shortcuts
Change between the present perspective and the true size	Input F9
Up- or down-scrolling	Press either the UP or DOWN arrow.
Sliding either left or right	Press either the LEFT or RIGHT arrow.
Upward scrolling in broad strokes	Press the UP arrow key or PAGE UP.
large-scale downward scrolling	Press the DOWN arrow key or PAGE DOWN.
large-scale leftward scrolling	Simply press CTRL+LEFT ARROW.
large-scale rightward scrolling	CTRL + RIGHT ARROW
Getting to the page's upper left corner when scrolling	Click: HOME
Getting to the page's bottom right corner by scrolling	Click: END
the Go To Page dialog box being shown	Hit F5 or CTRL+G. Hit CTRL+PAGE UP.
the previous page	Then, press CTRL+PAGE DOWN.
the following page	Input: CTRL+F6
visit the following window (if you have multiple publications Opening)	Input: CTRL+P
Displaying the Print view after exiting Print Preview	Input: Escape key
Turn off Print Preview	Input F9

Print a publication shortcut

Actions	Shortcuts
Opening the Print dialog view.	Press: CTRL+P

Inserting hyperlinks

Actions	Shortcuts
showing the dialog box for adding links (Making sure your cursor is in a text box)	Press: CTRL+K

Send an email shortcuts

The following keyboard shortcuts can be used after Selecting Send as Message **(File > Share > Email).**

Before you may send email messages, Outlook must be Opened. The mail will be kept in your Outbox folder if Outlook isn't Opening.

Actions	Shortcuts
Send the most recent issue or page	Input: ALT+S
the Address Book is opened (cursor must be in the message header)	Ctrl+Shift+B is pressed.
the Design Checker being opened (cursor must be in the message header)	Input: ALT+K
examining the To, Cc, and Bcc lines for names (cursor must be in the message header)	Input: CTRL+K
launching the Address Book while selecting the To box (cursor must be in the message header)	the ALT+ key (period)

launching the Address Book while selecting the Cc box (cursor must be in the message header)	Input: ALT+C
Accessing the Address Book and selecting the Bcc box (cursor must be in the message header and the Bcc field must be visible)	Input: ALT+B
Visit the Subject section.	Press ALT + J and ALT + P.
the Outlook Message Options dialog box being opened	Ctrl+Shift+G is pressed.
A custom dialog box is opened to establish an email message flag (cursor must be in the email message header)	Toggle: TAB
the next field in the email message header with the mouse (the cursor must be in the email message header)	Tap SHIFT+TAB.
Place your cursor in the email message header's preceding field.	Input: CTRL+TAB
Switch back and forth between the Send button in the Mailing toolbar and the Insertion point in the email message header.	Ctrl+Shift+B is pressed.
when the cursor is in the email message header, opening the Address Book	Press ALT + J and ALT + P.